Seized
by
Grace

Larissa Kay Ellis

ISBN 979-8-89112-164-5 (Paperback)
ISBN 979-8-89112-165-2 (Digital)

Covenant Books
11661 Hwy 707
Murrells Inlet, SC 29576
www.covenantbooks.com

Contents

Preface

This book came into being because of those who kept saying, "You must write a book!" Receiving three encouragements in one week, including from a new priest friend, I realized that God was trying to tell me something, and I obediently began writing.

Thank you, dear ones, for the final push. Without you three, these pages would still be unwritten, waiting in a corner of my heart to be brought into the light.

This is a true story of a lifetime's journey with a God that defies pat descriptions. Though most of the locations are vague, and all names are changed (including my own) to protect the privacy of others, the actual events are completely true and told without exaggeration.

This book is for everyone climbing the mountain to heaven. Whether you are unaware of the mountain, jumped off in your youth, are newly introduced to church and Jesus, well on your way up the mountain, rejoicing in a sweet spot, struggling with overwhelming circumstances, stuck in a rocky patch and unable to advance—or have walked away from the mountain altogether, there is a chapter here for you—not necessarily with answers but, rather, windows that heaven can peek through and speak directly to your heart. This book is not an instruction manual or a self-help book. It is a book of stories. True stories. *God* stories. Stories that show His presence before we know He is present, and ones that delight in the ways He shows up in a life...over and over and over again.

From the beginning, we were first and foremost a people of stories and testimonies borne out of personal experiences. The original twelve that walked so long ago in the company of Jesus joyfully shared their stories amidst persecution, in the end accepting martyrdom rather than denying the story written in their hearts. Their stories are remembered, permanently written with those of Jesus in the Book. *The Bible.*

We have become distracted, busy, weary—sometimes to the point of forgetting our own stories. We have watched others betray their stories, family members that faltered so badly that we question the very existence of a good God. Over time, many have shared their stories less and less, fearful of judgment, dismissing them as personal or unimportant, and the body of Christ has been less because of it. Stories lift up, encourage, engender hope—make us realize that we are not alone—and that others have walked in dark places too and survived. Thrived. Become victorious. Our stories must be shared.

It is my hope and prayer that as you read my story, *your* story will come alive in you—that you will see things you have not seen before, that you will notice all the places where God interceded (*and whether or not you were able to accept the grace offered at the time*), that you will know how deeply you are sought after and *loved* by the Father.

Book 1

Chapter 1

———

The Princess

Every story has a beginning and an end. Mine began with my birth to a mother who was raised during the Great Depression in a Catholic orphanage. She was as cool and matter of fact to her children as the nuns had been to their charges. Love was not absent, merely unde-monstrated and understood. She met my father straight out of the orphanage at eighteen and married him six months later. He was a truly brilliant man, bigger than life, charming, kind, loving, and generous to all.

Except when he wasn't.

There was a dark streak of pain and anger in my father that occasionally rose like a summer storm, blocking the sun, filling our skies with unexpected bolts of lightning and terrifying peals of thunder. I was his chosen child, the only girl with four younger brothers, his little princess—and though I knew that—his rage terrified me when the storms came in with thunderous, overwhelming blackness, crushing my brothers in front of me. Though I was terrified of the thunder, lightning never once struck the princess.

I adored him.

My memories from childhood are few. Bits and pieces, flashes of places, people, pets that disappeared as we moved more often than most. Rarely did we stay anywhere longer than a year. We were living in Canada the first time *God* showed up. I was in second grade in a Catholic parochial school, and our class had taken a field trip.

We had returned early; it was cold and snowy. A classmate's parent offered to bring me home, and shivering, I gratefully accepted. She dropped me off with a smile and a wave, waiting for me to open our front door. I realized Mom was not home the second I opened the door. In that moment, I remembered it was my father who was picking me up from school. I imagined him waiting for me, becoming angry, worried…and saw that this time, lightning might strike me after all! In fear, I dropped to my knees in front of my bedroom window and, eyes searching the gray skies, pleaded with God to save me! Moments later, I saw our neighbor walking in front of our house with his big black dog, and I ran outside into the cold, sobbing, begging for his assistance in my distress. He immediately drove me back to the school, and there was my father in the parking lot…waiting for me. He greeted me with a smile! I was *saved!*

Later, the neighbor told me that he had been sitting and watching TV with his dog sleeping at his feet. He had no idea why he had chosen to wake his dog up and take him for a walk at that exact moment. God had reached down, seized my neighbor, pulled him from his comfortable chair in front of a warm fire and sent him to rescue me!

I knew exactly why.

God had heard me.

Shortly after that, my father decided that the church was corrupt and unnecessary. We quit going to Mass, he pulled me out of parochial school, and God became a nonsubject in our lives as he went after the American dream, and we struggled with being children of the sixties. It took many years to become aware that my Heavenly Father continued to watch over and save me from others and myself.

Chapter 2

The Princess Walks in Darkness

My Parents' Darkness

All of us have darkness within us. Some is our own by virtue of our choices. Other bits are bequeathed to us by our parents, and other parts roll down generation to generation. My dad was a confusing enigma to me—a joyous, bantering jokester (whom I adored) who could turn into a terrifying tornado of rage without warning. We never knew when the change would occur, and we all learned to walk softly in his presence. There were mornings when we woke up to a quiet mother and a new hole in the wall or a shattered piece of furniture that had been whole the night before.

Running away at fourteen, misrepresenting his age to join the Marines during wartime, ending up in a prisoner of war camp, my father returned stateside, still plagued by the demons he had picked up in the war. Meeting my mother was a settling influence on him, and they found stability in each other. The Marine Corps and the war had moved him into adulthood, ingraining the belief that strong discipline was necessary to instill character. Corporal punishment was part of that picture. He was determined his sons would grow up to be "good men." There were times I would come home to one or more of my brothers face down on their bed, beaten for an infraction of the house rules.

I became "the good girl," careful not to break rules, and "yes, sir" came quickly to my lips. On the rare times he was at home, we all would desperately seek his company, desiring him to play with us, but fear was a shadow in the background of all our games. I became the family meteorologist—reading the skies around him, signaling when it was safe. I remember he was always teaching: Stick together as a family. Do not lie. *Ever.* Do not steal. *Ever.* Do not disobey. *Ever.* These rules were immutable.

Two times in my young life I was punished unfairly and harshly for rules I had not broken. The first was for a handprint on his pillowcase (falsely attributed to me) that enraged him so greatly that he reached out to destroy the one thing that was precious to me in retribution. I had gotten a stuffed life-sized mechanical kitten for my birthday that I loved as though it were real. Maybe in some ways it was real to me. I took her with me everywhere.

I heard Father's warning roar from the bedroom but did not scramble to my feet in time. As the sole available child, he caught me by the arm, marched me into the bedroom, swung his arm in the direction of the offending pillowcase, and bellowed, "Destroy something of *mine* and I will destroy something of *yours!*" Ripping my kitten from my arms, he tore off her head in his rage and threw the pieces to the ground. Pieces of my little heart fell too; my baby had been destroyed for something I didn't do, and there was nothing I could do to stop it.

The second time was several years later. This episode included all my brothers. We had been sent to the local five-and-dime to buy a toy balsa wood airplane as a reward for good behavior, with the instructions to bring it home without opening it. Our excitement was over the top! We laughed, played touch-tag, and skipped our way there, bubbling over in anticipation!

Once purchased, our curiosity drove us to peel open the resealable top and carefully peruse the contents, then, feeling guilty, we pushed it all back and resealed the tab. There was a certain thrill in our secret disobedience, and we ran the rest of the way home, jubilant. My father met us in the yard, received the purchased plane from our hands, and we sat down on the grass at his feet for the assembly process. Our elation was short-lived.

No, no, no… The propeller was missing! With a flinty look, he ascertained we had opened the package and sternly charged us to go back and find the missing piece. Suddenly, the day had turned deadly serious. We frantically retraced every step searching for the errant piece on which our fate was resting without success. Shamefaced and downcast we returned home empty-handed, and off we went, five distraught goslings following an angry silent gander, awaiting the impending doom. The finding of the piece was now irrelevant—punishment was unavoidable—but my little soul rebelled against the final judgment and the corporal punishment that followed.

He retraced our steps, found the piece, and pronounced the sentence: We would be punished for *lying*. For saying that we couldn't find the piece, when it obviously *was findable* since *he* found it! We trailed behind him as in a POW death-march, not knowing our fate, but knowing it would be terrible.

It was.

Trembling, we were lined up in our shared bathroom. He purposefully cut the blue bar of soap in the soap dish into five pieces, commanding us to eat them. We ate as commanded—gagging and drooling as we swallowed the frothing bits of blue. He sent us wide-eyed and nauseous to our rooms. *I got so, so sick.* I felt feverish and still remember the color of the wall and how cool its pale blue felt against my face as I pressed against it. The hardest part for me was not the soap; it was being punished for *lying*. I did not lie. A spanking for being disobedient would have been just. Eating soap for a lie I did not tell broke something inside of me.

We were too sick to eat dinner that night and did not enter the land of the living until midday the next day. The ill-fated plane was assembled and broken in two in the trash as a reminder of our transgression. I learned a lesson that day, but not the one my father had tried to teach.

I learned I could not resist someone stronger than me.

I learned I had no voice.

Those lessons would haunt my teens and young adulthood. And they defined me in ways I did not understand; my voicelessness changing the direction and course of my life. Evil can easily take advantage of those kinds of lessons, and as it does with many, so it did with me. I was easily bullied, especially by the men in my life. I didn't know how to get out or say "no." Both cost me dearly.

My Darkness

Rather than tell the story of my journey through darkness in detail, I wish only to reveal enough that you understand I was not special or particularly protected from the harsh realities of the world. My inability to speak up for myself exacted a high price: my virginity, my right to refuse, being drawn into situations not of free choice, and a deep depression that drove me close to suicide more than once. I was not religious. I did not pray. I was merely trying to survive.

The next time God intervened in my life, I was sixteen. I was on my way back to my high school after lunch when flashing lights appeared in my rearview mirror. My heart froze. My father would *kill* me if I came home with a ticket! I noted that it was not a police car and that the man getting out of it did not seem right. His look was smug and predatory. An interior voice commanded me, "Go! Drive to the school! *Do not stop!*"

Panicking, breath coming in gulps, I drove, flashing lights coming up behind me with a siren that *woop-wooped* on and off as he pursued. I came in sight of the high school and pulled into the Northside parking lot. He turned off his lights and siren and peeled away.

A call from the high school office to the local police department confirmed what my gut had told me—this was not an undercover policeman in an unmarked car. The seriousness of my situation did not become evident until the next day when it was reported that one of our female teachers had been murdered in her car on her way home that very afternoon. I had been the murderer's target number 1. I believe God had protected me—this time, without my knowing or asking.

That summer, driving home from an outing with a group of teenage friends, my fear was realized. We were stopped for speeding, and I was given a ticket. The shock and embarrassment kept me from crying all the way home, but once I got there, I absolutely fell apart! How could I tell my father?! *He would kill me.* I was truly terrified of what the outcome of this confession might bring. I didn't sleep. I ate little. I met my mother and brothers with distracted silence—each day, going over and over in my mind how this was going to play out—and not a single scenario ended well. Finally on day 6, my mother came to my room, sat on my bed, and gently demanded to know *what* was going on. I hemmed and hawed, cried and stalled, but eventually, the truth broke through; and I held my breath, waiting for her response.

"You will have to tell your father."

I panicked. *"I CAN'T!"* Terror washed over me.

"Couldn't *YOU* tell him *for* me?"

She adamantly refused. It was my ticket. I would have to tell him. I had a week to figure out how, as the ticket payment was coming due. All $312.

How could I tell him?! Thunder and lightning were sure to rage. I was terrified. I slept and ate even less and waited until the last moment possible to confront my father. I looked pale, thinner and with dark circles around my eyes, face swollen from crying, I'm sure I was quite the picture!

My father looked up from his work when I entered, slightly taken aback at my countenance and, tilting his head slightly, asked why I was there. I had avoided him for weeks, and now here I was face-to-face with all my fears taunting me. In that terrible moment, I told him that I had something I had to tell him and that I did not know how. He met my gaze and said, "Just *tell* me." I took a deep breath, gathered every ounce of courage I had left and poured it all out, speaking a mile a minute, sobbing between phrases, looking down at my feet, waiting for the axe to fall! The silence after my confession was deafening, and I began to tremble as tortuous thoughts tumbled through my head.

I heard my father's voice, soft and measured, incredulously say, "*Is that…all?!*" I nodded my head in affirmation and was totally unprepared for his next statement delivered with a huge smile: "If that is the worst thing you ever do, I will be a happy, happy man!"

I dropped my guard, realizing that I was not about to "die," and we hugged. A long, sweet, father-daughter hug that brought our relationship to an entirely new level. Never again was I afraid of him. It was as if we now had a secret covenant between us. It was not until years later that I learned why he had been so relieved by my confession. While I had agonized over *how* to *tell* him, the thought had seized him (an act of grace?) I could be *pregnant*…

No wonder that a ticket (even a $312 one) was a *relief* and good news to him indeed!

This protection would continue. Predatory men would show up on and off throughout my life, and each time, I would be seized by unmerited grace—pulled from utter destruction—though not from distress or from pain. I dabbled in the occult, "white" witchcraft, Ouija boards and tarot cards, looking for answers, finding none. The only reading I ever had done left the palm reader astonished at the amount of confusion and spiritual energies surrounding me. I played with those psychic energies and reveled in the teasing "powers" I found there—identifying cards before they were turned over, playing with white magic spells, moving objects with my thoughts, totally unaware that this was dangerous ground. His hand was already extended to grasp and pull me free.

At seventeen, I found myself in Spain in the early 1970s where I met a man who was to be my first experience with a loving relationship. I had experienced the horror of date-rape at sixteen and too many men after only one thing. This one was a good man. Decent. Kind. He showed me great kindness and a way of life that I had not known existed. Franco was ruling Spain with an iron fist at that time in history. His dictatorship affected all of society, including the lives of those visiting from other countries. We were welcome but sternly warned to be off the streets before 3:00 a.m. as the *Guardia Civil* would be patrolling from then until dawn, and they were known to shoot and ask questions later. A building had collapsed in town, and we had gone down to witness the damage, both of us profoundly affected by the loss of property and life. We went to a local bar and sat and talked late into the night—realizing a little too late that curfew was about to shut everything down. Driving home was out of the question.

Fortunately, he knew something I did not. There was an underground network of after-curfew places where the night-people descended to await the dawn. He led me quickly down a nearby alley to a stairwell leading to a windowless basement entry door. Knocking sharply three times elicited a small eye-level door sliding open. A code phrase was given, and the large wooden door swung open, welcoming us in to an amazing space. The walls and floor were stone. What windows there were, were all securely shuttered. The smell of baking bread and freshly brewed coffee filled the air, dancing between the tendrils of cigarette smoke. Tables were packed side by side and filled with smiling people. Huge serrano hams hung like ornaments from the ceiling, and platters of hot bread, ham, and cheese graced almost every table. The room rang with laughter and vibrated with the murmur of intense conversation—I had never seen anything like it; I felt like I had walked into a Humphrey Bogart movie!

We drank coffee, ate warm homemade bread with thick slices of salty ham, and talked until morning. Finally, we spilled out into the street at dawn to find the sun coming up over the ocean in a glorious display of color. Fishing boats pulled ashore as the sunrise tinted the sands a soft pink. Fishermen brought in their catch of sardines and roasted them over open charcoal fires. Ladies in black stirred vats of hot chocolate and fried-up churros. We sat on the sea wall enjoying these offerings and watched the sun rise into the new day.

It was a sweet time in my life; instinctively, I knew this man was trustworthy, and as that sun came up warming us on that seawall, we both willingly fell deeper into this new relationship. After a short courtship, he asked me to marry him, and being young and thoroughly smitten, I said *yes*.

I followed him back to his home country where we lived temporarily with his sister and her husband then moved in with friends near the city center. Slowly, over time, I began to realize that my personality overwhelmed his, and that if we married, I might well become an old shrew and he a browbeaten old man—a thought that sobered me as I knew he deserved better, and so did I. He was a gentle soul who deserved a gentle woman. I would need a much stronger man to match forces with. I was not yet used to kindness.

One evening, we were invited to go with our friends to a party in the city. It was a cold, drizzly night, and we entered the huge foyer of the rather grand host house, taking off our coats and preparing to join the gathering. Almost immediately, we were shocked by a loud, very authoritarian voice coming from a striking figure at the head of the tall staircase. Looking down on us, her voice rang out, silencing the room: "*You!*" We turned to look up at her. Her face was intense, her piercing eyes fierce, indescribable. She was pointing directly at *me.*

"Yes! *You! You do not belong here! What is here will destroy you…you are not strong enough!*" Her voice intensified into a firm, indisputable command: "Get out! Now!"

To this day, I do not know if she was a guardian angel or a guardian witch or just seized by the hand of God. All I know is that instant became a defining moment in my life. Her words stopped us at the door and drove us out. We were stunned and left quickly. Later, it was revealed that the "party" had been a gathering of a rather large coven of witches, and its hostess had been the one to "see" me and command us to leave. Fifty years later, my heart still freezes at the memory.

I summarily dropped all psychic activity. Frightened by the intensity of her comments and disillusioned by my unbalanced relationship, I broke off the engagement to the man and returned to Spain. Restless and unable to find peace there, I journeyed to Rota to join the United States Navy. It was near the end of the Vietnam Era, and they were delighted to sign me up as a medic. I was off, back to the States—courtesy of the United States Government—heading to boot camp and corpsman (HM) training immediately after. I had no idea of what I was getting into, just what I was getting *out* of; can you say "frying pan into the fire!?"

Boot camp was a huge wake-up call, and corps school became a clarion call to engage my newfound passions for the medical field and of all things—singing, *gospel singing*. One of my boot camp buddies loved to play guitar and sing of God's goodness wherever she went, and I found that I loved it too. I did not yet fully understand this "ole time religion" God we sang about, but I loved his story and the good things that happened to me when I was immersed in it with her.

We had many sweet adventures together, but one that sticks in my memory is the cab ride we took from the airport in 1973 to "A" School, coming out of boot. The cabbie spotted her guitar case and asked if she played "that thing." She responded with an emphatic "Yes! But we only play and sing Gospel music!" He looked a little surprised but shrugged and came back with "I guess that'll be okay." The guitar came out of his trunk, and we piled into the back seat. We sang of God's goodness, we sang of being lost and being found, and we sang songs of redemption. Every once in a while, I would catch him looking intently at us in the rearview mirror. As we sang songs of joy over the thirty-five-minute journey, our voices dancing in sweet harmonies, his face began to soften.

We finally arrived, got out, got our luggage and guitar case from the trunk, and turned to pay him the $75 fare. He took the money, turned it in his hand, and passed it back saying that he couldn't take it. What we had given to him over the last thirty-five minutes in God-song had deeply impacted him and was worth *far* more than those dollars to him. He then became very serious and counseled us to remember something that *he had forgotten*—that God was always present—even when we could not *feel* Him! He gently reminded us, though we obviously were basking in His Presence now, a time would come when we would not feel Him, and to remember *then* what he was saying now: "GOD IS STILL THERE. *Regardless of what you* FEEL. *Hold onto that.*"

We were jubilant. God had spoken to his heart through our music, and I decided then and there that singing for the Lord was an awesome privilege! Forty years would pass before I would recall his words to us and hold on to them with everything that I had in me. We sang our way through our time in corps school and were often gifted with free meals in restaurants, free beverages in bars, and of course, free cab rides. It was a lovely time of soaking in His goodness!

Once we graduated and moved to our first duty station, life proceeded to get very messy, and it became apparent that I was not good at getting out of bad situations that tended to wrap around my life like tentacles of an octopus—one arm loosening, another wrapping tighter. Again, in a protective act, *God freed me.*

Chapter 3

The Protector

At the age of twenty-five, I believe He sent a soldier to protect me. A marriage was arranged (long story), and though I did not know what love was with the chosen one, I sensed he would be a safe haven for me…and he was. We were married in the Catholic Church. On my return from an eight-week training deployment to a military hospital to become a physician's assistant, I got pregnant. It had not been planned, but we were happy about it. My mom was excited at the prospect of becoming a grandmother, and it felt very much in the natural order of things. I unexpectedly miscarried at five months and grieved hard for what had been lost. The grief was made more difficult by the fact that in those days, stillborn babies were thrown away and the mother's loss pretty much dismissed. I held him in my womb but never in my arms. Months later, I regrouped; and silently, I held him in my heart, mourned his loss, and named him Eric Scott.

I got pregnant again a year later, and this one I carried to term. The funny part was, as long as I was pregnant, I felt very loving and close to my husband. After delivery, everything changed. It did not help that I had nearly died during childbirth and was deathly afraid of getting pregnant again. I'd had a long labor, and they had decided to do a C-section if things did not progress. I decided, heck no—this baby was coming out the way God intended, and I started pushing with everything I had in me! I broke all the blood vessels in my eyes, one in my face and one in my neck. I looked like I had been hit by a

Mack Truck, but I pushed that baby out! After my delivery, the inexperienced military doctor literally pulled my uterus out of my body, trying to rush things along and then froze, not knowing what to do. I proceeded to bleed to death. They quickly ushered my husband out of the delivery room and sent the baby to the nursery. The pain was incomprehensible. All I wanted to do was die so that the pain would stop. At the precise moment, they rang code blue, the head of Obstetrics walked into the military hospital and ran upstairs to the delivery room. Coming in early to do some paperwork, he did not expect to be met by a code blue! The head doctor came in barking orders as he gowned and gloved up and, though he had never seen this situation before, assumed the right protocol, and I lived. Six units of whole blood, with the AIDS epidemic announced shortly after, kept me in a state of worry for nearly four years until we were sure I had not contracted it from the transfusions. A uterus coming out? Who knew *that* could even happen!?!

I was so traumatized by the experience and the news that while it was very rare as a first-time occurrence and usually connected with due cause (in my case, the prolonged labor and the doctor trying to pull the placenta out via traction) the odds went up in subsequent pregnancies, and it could be spontaneous (without cause). *Yikes!* I was terrified of getting pregnant again. A spirit of fear grabbed hold, and after six months of avoidance my husband and I agreed to get my tubes tied to try to get back to a semblance of normalcy. Fear is a terrible thing. That decision led us out of the Catholic Church and into a nearby Episcopalian Church located on the water. I felt God's presence there, and we were welcomed. Their priest was generous, seeing us privately, hearing our story and offering support. He even gave us his phone number "in case of emergency." Little did I know, I would actually *need* it.

I began going to a community college using the GI Bill I had earned during my military service, studying arts and science. During a course presented as World Religions, I found myself under attack by a professor for "buying" the Christian story and elevating it above all the others. Though I still did not understand this God or His rules well, I felt He existed, that He intervened in our lives, and I boldly said so. The professor sniffed, some of my classmates laughed, but I did not back down—God had shown up too many times in my life to deny Him now. Later, a young lady came up to ask me if I *really* believed that God was real, and when I assured her I did, she asked me to meet her that afternoon.

We met in a quiet place on campus and as the water feature next to us bubbled cheerily, her story unwound, and my blood ran cold. Goosebumps made their way across my arms, and a serpentine shiver shot up my spine. She had come from the west coast. She had been involved with witchcraft and the occult. Scary events started occurring after engaging in the occult there, enough to cause her to fear for her life. She panicked and left. Thinking she could run from it, she had crossed all the way to the other side of the country, ending up on the east coast, only to find that she had not outrun it at all.

She was living with a new boyfriend who would leave for work at four o'clock every morning. One morning after he left, she was awakened at exactly five thirty-five by a deeply disturbing dream where she saw a pig with red eyes running through her house and dead animals nailed to her walls almost as though they were crucified. Out the window, she noticed two punk rocker-looking young people in front of her house. She awoke to a coldness in the room she had never experienced before and an evil dark presence above her, pressing her down onto the bed. She felt as though she, her very soul, was in mortal danger. She was terrified. It disappeared.

The next night, she tried to stay awake after her boyfriend left but fell asleep and again dreamed. The dream was similar, but this time, it was a weasel with burning red eyes running through her house, knocking things over, breaking things up. It felt malevolent, and when she awoke (again, at exactly five thirty-five), the room was freezing cold, and a dark, intensely evil presence stood at the foot of her bed. Terrified, she lay there until it disappeared.

She trembled as she recounted her story. Although my experience with the occult was limited to a little white magic, a single encounter with the witches coven overseas and a paper on demonology I had written for a college class; I had no doubt that she was speaking truth. I told her that I knew a priest that I could talk to, gave her a hug, and encouraged her with the hope I could find answers.

The irony was, the priest that had provided me with his number had also led me to believe through previous conversations that he would know what to do. God had already been putting pieces into place for my new friend's benefit. He had used my pain and fear to connect me with this particular priest, my college class to open the door of conversation on this particular subject. This priest graciously assisted by sharing personal encounters with evil during my research on demonology for my class paper, and we had long discussions on the subject. Due to those conversations, I actually had the foresight to ask some pertinent questions after her harrowing story had been relayed.

Unfortunately, when I called, he was on sabbatical on the other side of the state, so he was not free to come, but like me, he felt convicted by her story and was willing to instruct and assist us from a distance. I was able to tell him that she was unbaptized, no family had been involved in the occult; and detailed the trip from the west coast, the dreams, the freezing cold, the feeling of doom, and the dark presence.

He took a deep breath and asked me where my daughter was. (She was staying with her grandmother.) Relieved, he began to outline what I could do to help. He told me to go to a Catholic Church to get holy water, a blessed candle, and the rite of baptism. Apparently, a layperson is permitted to baptize someone in mortal danger, and if I could get those items, he would give me the code to the sanctuary of his church, and I could bring her there to baptize her! Until then, he asked if I had a rosary I could give her to wear for protection. I did not. I went to a store, purchased a small sterling silver rosary in a lovely little pouch, and tucked it into my purse.

I went to a Catholic church nearby, and actually found a priest in the foyer. I told him the story, and his shock was palpable. He declared that he did not believe in personified evil but could not deny the effect my story had on his spirit and was not willing to risk denying me what I asked for. He provided the holy water, blessed candles, and the rite of baptism. I met my new friend, gave her the rosary, and told her that my priest said if the entity returned, she was to command it to leave in the *Name of Jesus Christ*. We then made arrangements to meet at the Episcopalian church at 6:00 p.m. the next night.

The phone rang at 4:00 a.m. It was my little friend, and she was terrified. Breathing erratically and crying, speaking in broken sobs, she recounted how the dark presence had shown up again. This time, there was no dream, the entity just woke her up by grabbing her throat, throttling her, breaking the rosary I had given her into three pieces. She tried with all her might to say the name of Jesus but could not open her mouth to speak. All of a sudden, she heard angelic voices command the spirit to *leave in the Name of Jesus Christ!* Instantly, the dark hand released, and the entity disappeared. I reassured her (my own heart pounding in my chest) the presence would not come back, that she would be baptized that very evening, and that I believed that sacrament would stop the attacks for good. My God was stronger than her darkness.

I immediately called the priest even though it was only 4:15 a.m. and found him awake and praying. *He had been fasting and praying since my first call.* He had been awakened at 3:00 a.m. and had been on his knees praying ever since, asking that warrior angels would be sent to protect my friend. When I told him what had happened, he wept for joy at the goodness of the God he served! I believe this priest in his obedience and his nighttime prayer *sent the angels to speak the words* my friend could not! He did warn that the baptism could bring on a spiritual battle depending on how big the spirit we were up against actually was. We were willing to take the risk.

That evening, we met at the church. My new friend told me that her car acted up all the way there. The radio wouldn't work, and she stalled out at every stop. It was crazy. Those things had never happened before, and she felt like something didn't want her to get there. The interesting part is, after the baptism, her car was fine; the radio worked perfectly. No stalling.

It was late fall, so the sun was already drawing low in the sky, and the light in the sanctuary was dim. The air was still, the church quiet, and the evening light shone through the magnificent stained-glass windows as though heaven were watching us. We sat on the steps in front of the altar. I read the rite of baptism and baptized her in the name of the Father, and of the Son and of the Holy Spirit while pouring the holy water over her head. As we prayed the final prayer, we both realized something extraordinary had happened. The air around us was rarefied, the light golden, and we were wrapped in a warmth that defied description! Neither one of us wanted to leave, and we sat there for a very long time. *A very long time.* It was dark by the time we walked out of the church into the salty night air. Crickets were singing in the old live oaks along the river, and we looked up at the radiant stars knowing heaven was smiling! I went home rejoicing.

That night, my newly baptized friend decided to prepare ahead for the night to come. She got up when her boyfriend left. Lighting the two blessed candles I had given her, she opened her Bible and sat up in bed waiting. She did not have to wait long. The room became *frigid.* She noticed her bed move, as though someone had leaned onto it, and watched as a large dark figure manifested at the foot of the bed. A foul smell permeated the room, and the figure malevolently leaned in close but apparently could not break the blessed circle of light emanating from the candles, stopping at the edge created by light encroaching the darkness. Bravely, she leaned forward and Bible in lap, in a strong authoritative voice commanded the spirit to *"Leave in the Name of Jesus Christ and never come back!"*

The effect was immediate and startling. The air was clean.

It never came back.

That was forty-two years ago. We are still in touch. She is still a "God girl." Through all of this, though he did not participate, my husband was supportive. The experience drew us both back into the Catholic Church as that is where the rite and sacramentals had come from, and I figured if God could stop a demon, He could fix me.

A one-year unaccompanied deployment out of the country for my husband moved me and our daughter to stay with my father and his new wife. That same year, my mother moved out of state to be close to her sister. On my husband's return from overseas, we separated, and he took our daughter while I figured out what I was going to do. I tried moving to a nearby city on my own to find employment to support myself, intending to make our separation permanent. It did not go well.

I was on my own. My naivety became apparent. The search for a job took longer than expected, and my funds began to run out. I vowed not to eat until I had a job and money coming in. I needed all the cash I had for rent and gas. I was down to a mere ninety-nine pounds when I entered a roadside diner and hungrily sat at the counter watching the short order cook flip burgers and drop fries. He cheerfully asked what he could get me, and I countered back with a cheery "Just a coffee, please."

I still remember his earnest face. I guess he could tell I was hungry, because moments after the coffee was poured, a hot fragrant grilled cheese sandwich appeared in front of me. Surprised and slightly distressed, I told him, "I can't *pay* for that—the budget says *coffee!*"

To which he replied, "No payment necessary. It's on me. Someday, you will pay it forward for somebody else. It's all good... enjoy it!"

We chatted as I devoured the glorious sandwich, cheese dripping onto the plate below. I would never forget this kindness. Best of all, as I left, he gave me a lead on a job waiting tables, and I was hired that very day! I think maybe the restaurant manager hired me out of pity, as I had no previous experience, and each shift started with a meal that she insisted I eat before I went out on the floor. A small breakfast joint in a shopping center was the perfect starting place for me. The clientele were kind and patient as I learned the ropes, and I got better and better with time. I actually *liked* the job, and I loved my boss-lady!

I found myself struggling to understand this God I kept encountering. This God that drove away demons, served up cheese sandwiches, directed me to employment, got me hired, and fed me daily. After a few months on my own, His grace seized me once again, bringing me back to my husband and daughter for another five years of protection.

It was during this time that I learned my mom was dying of lung cancer. My husband's sister dropped everything and came to watch our daughter. I flew to the west coast, and Mom and I began to walk that three-month journey from diagnosis to death together. God loved us even in our mother-daughter brokenness. We walked hand in hand. We had long talks. *She* hugged *me*. Growing up, I had hugged her—but could not remember *her* ever hugging me. Sharing a room, we laid in the shadowed stillness of the night, and I would awaken to the sound of rosary beads passing through her fingers and her quiet conversations with God between the Our Fathers and Hail Marys.

Three weeks before she died, my husband insisted I come home. My mom was crushed; I felt guilty if I stayed, guilty if I left. My husband sounded so desperate I chose to leave. In retrospect, I should have stayed. I missed her last two good weeks, and by the time they called me to come she was worn out by the battle and uncommunicative. Her only words broken up by short gasping breaths: "You shouldn't…have come…I don't…need…you now…" My guilt rose within my breaking heart to level ten. That guilt dug in hard and opened the final door that would lead to divorce from my husband.

Mom was admitted to the hospital run by the same sisters that had looked after her in the orphanage. Mother Cabrini was at her beginning and there for her in the end. One of the elderly nuns remembered her "little girl" and came to visit her daily until she passed. I stayed by her bedside refusing to leave, wanting desperately to stay awake to be fully present in her last hours. I kept falling asleep, head dropping to my chest, only to be shocked back to consciousness by a gasp or soft cry, and waves of guilt would wash over me yet again.

The morning of her passing, the agonizing struggle to breath eased, her mind became clear, and she called for the family to come in and say "goodbye." She knew she was leaving. I helped her wash her face, brush her teeth, and comb her hair before she held her final court. I was the last one to receive her blessing, and as I leaned over, to my great surprise, she reached up and tweaked my nose—*hard!* Chuckling mischievously, her eyes twinkling with a light I had never seen before, she authoritatively declared with a wave of her hand, "You will *not* forget *this* goodbye!" She was right. I never have.

Laying back into the hospital pillow, her body relaxed. The tightness in her face disappeared, and she just stopped breathing. I cried out in distress—her eyes opened, she took a ragged breath, and I relented—quickly giving her permission through my tears to leave! One more breath, and she was gone. At that moment, I felt a presence in the hospital room, and I saw the first real smile wash over her face as she moved into eternity! *I felt her leave.* My life was still a mess, but I had hope that this God I kept encountering was real, and with *Him* one day all *could* change.

Chapter 4

The Shift

Feeling completely broken and lost after the death of my mom, still struggling with the guilt of leaving her, I walked through isles of Mother's Day cards that May with an overwhelming sense that *I was now the orphan.* My eyes burning with tears, my heart thudding inside of me: "*You...don't...have...a mother...!*" I felt lost. Emptied out. My dad was remarried and busy with his own life. I had no close friends. I felt totally alone.

My daughter's father and I both worked hard to connect, trying marriage encounter, counseling and declaring love for one another. We were kind, one to the other. None of it was enough to address my brokenness. My miscarriage at five months, nearly dying when my daughter delivered, the long recovery mixed with worry and fear generated by the trauma, then my mother's death and following depression, all took their toll. He was a good man. A good provider. I had tried to be a good mother, to keep a clean house while working evenings waiting tables to help with finances. We had a beautiful home, a loving daughter. We had pets. None of it was enough.

Despite our efforts, I was struggling as a wife and as a mother, and depression again began to raise its ugly head. Overwhelmed by all of life's realities, I finally asked for a divorce which was granted—as long as I gave full custody of our daughter over to him—a heart wrenching choice. The annulment process through the Church was complicated by rules and paperwork, but in the end, the tribunal decreed that a valid marriage had not occurred, and in mere months, we were both freed to move on with our lives.

He was a loving father, and he did keep his promise of granting me full access to our daughter, but it was difficult, nonetheless. I think people feel like divorce will solve so many problems (especially when they are deeply unhappy), but unfortunately, it carries with it a whole new set of issues, trauma, and pain that are totally unexpected. That was the case. For me. For him. For our daughter.

The first few years on my own were a difficult terrain to traverse in my naivete, and bad men reappeared to take advantage as they often do. Too many stories to relate and not the purpose of this book. Suicide again began to look like a valid option in my continued brokenness. I went to church. I tried to pray, but God seemed so far away. My theology was patchwork at best, and though, I was no longer enamored with New Age religions, mainstream Christianity did not draw me either. I had seen too many label themselves "Christian" that would make Christ shudder, and use the name of "JE-SUS!" in such a way that even the name somehow sounded ugly in their mouths! Catholicism felt cold and closed, like a club I no longer belonged to. I so wanted to find this elusive God, but it seemed the waters just kept getting murkier and murkier the more I tried. As the darkness once again overwhelmed, a place for the light to break through appeared in the most inopportune place. A new job.

I had gone from inexperienced waitress in a breakfast joint, to a competent server at a chain restaurant, moving on to a large bar and grill on the riverfront. I was working there when my divorce came through. It was there on the outside deck that I watched with other patrons the ill-fated launch of the Space Shuttle Challenger on January 28, 1986. The morning was icy cold and after a few delays she eventually took to the sky, shooting up in a glorious arc for a full seventy-three seconds. I watched in horror as a huge exploding column of white smoke appeared, and I was hit with an interior impression of terror and silent screams. While others were questioning exactly what they were seeing, I knew. The shuttle was going down. The grill closed in mourning for all who died, including the first civilian, a schoolteacher, Christa McAuliffe. I went home in shock to process what I had seen and heard. I did not return to work for nearly two weeks. I did not know how I had connected to what was going on so high above me in the shuttle cabin as it blew away from the plane. Or why I felt their fear and "heard" their brief cries before the crew cabin plummeted silently down into the ocean.

In those days, I did not yet know anyone else that felt, heard, or saw the kinds of things I did, and being so different was very isolating. So many changes all at once: my mother dying, my divorce, the change in parenting dynamics, and now this overwhelming inexplicable sensory event. I left the job at the bar and grill shortly after the Challenger disaster to distance myself from the memories and begin a totally new life many miles away. I accepted a job at a more formal Hilton dining room on the beach. The change in venue helped immensely.

One day, driving down a beach road, I decided to find a lunch spot and treat myself to a meal out. I came upon a little gem tucked among the trees and surrounded by gardens that I had not noticed before. It was glorious! I parked, walked in, and was instantly taken in by the magic of the interior. The artwork, the music, the light, the unbelievably beautiful gardens and mango trees. The staff called it "mango mystique."

All I knew is that I wanted to work there. I wanted to be part of that magic.

That magical restaurant was home and family to all that worked there, and joining their staff gave me the reason to live again. The restaurant life became my life; I was all in. I loved all of it. My coworkers, my bosses, the exacting nature of the job in a four-star establishment. The hustle and bustle and attention to detail was the perfect foil to my self-absorption. I was finding out what I was capable of and quickly rose in the ranks, becoming one of the top earners.

In my married life, I had returned to the Catholic Church of my childhood, and I had jumped into the religion wholeheartedly trying to connect with the God I remembered from my childhood. I enrolled in their programs, taught children's classes, went on retreats trying hard to become the good wife. With the failure of my marriage, I felt I had failed the church too, and my relationship with

Church and God became fragmented. I had missed something integral about God and who He was that made it easier to turn away than stay. My work became my family and my Church.

The time had come to make the move closer to the job that had become my life, and I found a lovely little condo a block from the beach that called my name! The week before I was to move in, my roommate-to-be abandoned the idea to move back with her parents, and I was stuck! Deposits had been made, rent was due on the first, and I did not have it. I was determined to make it happen. That night at end of shift; when all the staff were chatting easily in the back polishing glasses and silverware, my answer came to me. I literally heard a voice in my head saying, "Just *ask*." I latched onto that moment of grace, and without hesitation, I blurted out, "Who here would like to live in a very nice condo near the beach?"

A young, very bald, quiet waiter (whom I had dubbed the invisible man) answered as quickly as I had asked, saying, "I would be interested in getting out of the barracks."

He was newly divorced, a military guy and totally nonthreatening.

We met the next day for lunch, and he passed my interview with flying colors. I felt comfortable in his presence, and best of all, I was certain the fact that he was male would not be a problem as I was not in the least attracted to him. After so many failed relationships and unhappy encounters with men, I had actually begun to entertain the idea that perhaps loving a *woman* would be easier! I had already sworn off dating. Told God I was done. To keep it platonic with this man would be a cinch. Yep, I had a new roommate—the invisible man was my answer to an unspoken prayer.

Unexpectedly, without further fanfare, the next book of my life began.

Book 2

Chapter 5

A New Paradigm

The invisible man (now paid roommate) moved in three days later, coming in late after a shift at the restaurant. He silently entered the living room as *The Johnny Carson Show* filled the air with canned laughter. I hurriedly rose from my reclined position on the couch only to be waved back down with a "No, no, no—you were there *first!*" He sat gingerly at the foot of the couch, and we proceeded to watch Johnny's comedic renditions together, laughing easily and adding our own bits of off-the-cuff humor in between the scripted monologue.

Still not sure to this day what led up to it or how it happened, but this up-till-now invisible man *kissed* me. KISSED me! I literally saw *fireworks* just like in the movies, and at the ripe old age of thirty-three, thought to myself *this* is what a *real kiss* feels like… My next thought was I am going to *marry* this man. His name was John. John the beloved. John *my* beloved. This was the man I had been created to love in this lifetime.

No wonder I had never firmly connected to any of the others—no wonder I had questioned my own sexuality—I was made for *this* man. I was made to LOVE *this one!* I entered into the mystery.

It took him a year to say "I LOVE YOU." But once he did, I knew he meant it. Six months later—after a rocky passionate roller coaster relationship—he finally asked me on Christmas morning in the presence of my daughter if I would marry him—yes, yes…YES!

31

Our courtship had been tumultuous, both of us tripped up by the baggage we carried from our previous marriages. Yet somewhere in the midst of the messiness, God gave me a picture of what this broken angry man would look like "*if I loved him IN HIM.*" That image was enough to keep me hanging on in the middle of the worst storms. And there were many. He was not an easy man to love.

Protective miracle number 3:

I was driving a circuitous route through the mountains of Colorado between Durango and Pagosa Springs on our way home from a family reunion. Tight switchbacks, steep inclines, and treacherous drop-offs kept me focused on the road. Unexpectedly, I was faced with an impossible choice: go over the drop off thousands of feet down or hit a semitruck head on. A man in a dark sedan had decided to pass the semi on a curve, then laughing at us, eyes glowing red, he leaned into his steering wheel forcing me to make what he surely intended to be "my last decision." My husband-to-be cried out under his breath "God! We're going to die!" and ducked his head as I gripped the wheel, knuckles and face white. Suddenly, a great calm overtook me, and I heard an interior voice quietly instruct me to "go for the hole in the middle," understanding immediately that I was to aim for the space between the semi and the oncoming car. I whipped through the space with mere inches to spare on each side, my car shuddering in the wind tunnel created by the giant truck as we passed through the gauntlet of death unscathed.

What neither of us knew was that there was a third party in our relationship. An unholy one, and it hated me. With a passion. There were times that it would literally step in and take over—saying and doing things my beloved would never say or do…crushing me in ways I had never imagined possible. It was like being married to Dr. Jekyll and Mr. Hyde, never knowing when Mr. Hyde would appear, upending and destroying our peace. For many years, we both thought it was simply an unresolved anger issue, until one day, it became clear that anger was only the door "it" used to enter. We came face-to-face with the reality of a demonic entity. I've often wondered if it was one of its companion spirits driving the dark man we met in the mountains.

It took another twenty years to figure it out, call it by name, and command it to leave. We had lived under oppression for nearly twenty-five years without understanding its "otherness" or seeing clearly what actually was happening. To our credit, once we became aware and learned enough to call it out, the power was broken and after the third time of revoking all rights and permissions and commanding it to go—the entity never returned.

Now, back to *this* story.

Our three years of courtship led us back to the Rocky Mountains, where we both found work as servers at a family ski resort. Engaged for well over a year, I was beyond excited when one night, out of the blue, after a long heart-to-heart talk—we finally set *the date*. It was a done deal! We were getting *married!* All of a sudden, nothing else mattered, not the wedding format, the cake, not even the dress. When asked questions about wedding details by my coworkers at the resort we worked at, I would respond with "I don't know…but he is *marrying me!*" Slowly but surely the wedding took on a life of its own, as bosses, coworkers, and friends came forward and offered their assistance. A dress was given, a ribbon belt made to match for the occasion, a beautiful light gray tuxedo found. Our sous chef offered to bake our wedding cake as her gift to us, another couple donated flowers, another offered to do my hair and makeup, and the pianist that played on weekends at the restaurant offered to play Pachelbel's Canon in D for our wedding march. The resort owner offered their gorgeous banquet hall with a huge fireplace for our wedding ceremony. Friends and family made up the congregation. A Methodist minister presided.

My father had not come to my first marriage, but he was front and center this time. (He joked that he wanted to make sure this one "stuck"!) We said our vows in front of a blazing fire as the first snow of the season blanketed the ground outside. Our manager provided finger food and drinks for our small gathering of friends and family. Our sous chef's cake was an amazing white chocolate mousse masterpiece (elegantly decorated with real pink roses) that disappeared amid multiple sighs of "oh my goodness," with not a single crumb left to grace the platter. Wedding pictures were taken outside next to a carriage against a lovely white veil of snow. The first storm of the season that had threatened to block canyon roads and stop festivities became the perfect backdrop for the photos! The joy of our day was unmitigated. Our perfect unplanned wedding took shape by the sheer virtue of those who chose to participate in our Joy! It was *magnificent*.

As tumultuous as our courtship had been, marriage added its own dimensions of compromise and surprise. When we met, John had been a firm agnostic—he believed that there *was* a God, but not that He was involved with our lives. I could go to church if I wanted, but there was usually a disagreement of some kind on my return, so I learned early on to just stay home. The G-O-D word was not spoken, nor discussed between us and I figured that I could just pray on my own. As you can imagine, that choice did not play out well, and eventually, I was not praying at all.

One night, in the middle of the night, my new husband suddenly sat up, put his hand on my left breast, and cried out, "No, God! Don't take my baby from me!" Shocked by the outburst, I made an effort to rouse him—but he laid back in the bed sound asleep, not responding to anything I tried. Waking the next morning, I asked him directly, "What was last night about?!" and he responded that he did not recall waking up, crying out, or any particular dream, brushing off my questions, and all further conversation.

Three days later, I came home from a late shift at work to find him sitting up in bed with my Liturgy of the Hours Prayer Book (taken from my Hope Chest) in his lap. Startled by the incongruity of a prayer book in the lap of the man that refused to say the G-word I blurted out, "*What* are you *doing*?"

His response would forever change the course of our lives: "*I* REMEMBERED *the dream!* God came to me, telling me that I had taken You away from Him and that if I did not give you *back*, He would take you away from *me*."

He then went on to let me know that he had found a Catholic Church in the area, and that we would start going to church that Sunday. To say that I was shocked, surprised, and in disbelief would all be understatements. A switch had been flipped, and our whole world was about to be turned on its head. We had no idea what this change in direction would look like in lives that had not aligned with *God* previously, but we moved forward into it—blissfully ignorant of what was yet to come.

Chapter 6

The Fall into Grace

We entered a new season in more ways than one. Working the winter months in a ski resort brought a windfall of new money—lots of it—and we spent it as quickly as it came in. We reveled in the influx of celebrity icons and the cash that came with them, not knowing that the well would dry up come spring, and arid times were just around the corner. Poverty hit surprisingly hard.

We took in a roommate, worked double shifts, concerts, anything we could find to try and make up for lost wages, even moving to a cheaper place. Despite our efforts, each month the bills compounded, and it became necessary to consider other options to survive. By August, it became apparent that we weren't going to make it until the ski season again kicked in, and my husband decided to go back into the military. A visit to the local recruiter turned out to be a disappointment as the air force was in a recruiting slump and not willing to bring him back onboard. As he was walking out, a navy chief addressed him, asking, "Do you really want to get back in the military?" Snapping to attention, my husband answered with a sharp "Yes, sir!" and with a nod, he was invited into the recruiter's office. The navy didn't need anyone either, but this chief was committed to getting him back in. I never asked but wouldn't be surprised to find out he was a God-guy!

Eighteen hours of paperwork and waivers later, my husband was sworn in as an E-3 ready to report for reintegration training. We weren't sure what we were thinking or *how* we thought this was all going to work out. We still had a little rental house full of animals (two dogs, three cats) and few resources to fall back on. The week before he was set to report for duty, I bought a round-trip ticket for $75 to visit him while he was in training, without for a moment considering what I would do about all of our animals! When we are young, we are just so sure that "everything will just work out," and in this case—it *did*. God was working on it long before I even bought the ticket.

The Friday before he left, we worked a concert together, and at the end of the shift, were chatting with the bartender who was living out of her car with her toddler son. Internally, I heard, *"She's the one!"* understanding immediately that I was to make her an offer that she could not refuse. I told her of our dilemma and offered her a room in our little house rent-free for two months in exchange for her watching our animals while I was gone. She quickly accepted and moved in the day my husband left. I followed two weeks later.

Little did we know that I would never come back. Our lives had irreversibly shifted. Much farther down the road, we would realize that all of the pieces had been put in place long before we came to each junction, but "in the moment" we had no idea how completely God was orchestrating our steps as we moved forward into a future we could never have foreseen.

Arriving at the naval station, John was quickly processed in, but it took him ten days to realize that he had been put with "new recruits" instead of the reintegration program he had been slated for. Going before the captain got him transferred to the correct group, but not before he went through a class on self-checking for breast cancer—something that would become very important very quickly. I showed up at the airport four days later, and he picked me up in uniform—my handsome sailorman! We stayed the weekend with my stepmom. She was divorced from my father, but not from his kids, and we were welcome there.

That night the pieces started falling. As I curled up in the crook of his arm in the darkness, John discovered a large lump in my left breast (remember the dream?), and we both immediately knew it was not good. A trip to the naval hospital the next morning started what would end up being a long process in motion. They were unable to get me into the system quickly enough and referred me to a civilian doctor that had retired from the military several years earlier. My husband returned to training, and I moved in with my stepmom until we could figure everything out.

My new doctor's name was Dr. Armstrong, a fitting name for the man that would be proclaiming to my terrified soul about the strong arm of the LORD that would now unexpectedly manifest in my life. I went to his office on a Tuesday and was solemnly scheduled for surgery that Friday. He shook his head sadly as he examined me and let me know that despite my being only thirty-six, he was fairly certain that it was cancer. His suspicion proved correct, and a nurse friend of mine who assisted in the OR said he got tears in his eyes when he removed the tumor. The initial tests said cancerous, but it would be a week before we knew the kind and extent of this insidious intruder. I was nervous, but the gravity of my situation had not yet sunk into my spirit.

I was in a friend's condo on the beach when his phone call came.

"I have your results."

"Okay...," I said, measuring my words and tone carefully. "What are my numbers?"

His response surprised me. "I don't believe in numbers."

I quickly retorted with a small measure of irritation. "That's okay for *you* to say, but it is my life, and I would like to know what my odds are!"

He sighed deeply and said that he would tell me what my report said if I would listen to a story first. Good thing he could not see my *face* because the eye roll I gave was a doozy!

Reluctantly, I gave the go ahead, and the story began: He had been called in to counsel a woman that had been diagnosed with pancreatic cancer that morning. Entering her room, he quickly became aware that something else was going on besides the cancer and when he pressed her, she exploded in exasperation!

"I'll tell you what's going on! My daughter is pregnant with my first grandchild and is to deliver in seven months, and they have told me I am to die in *six*!"

Gently, he responded with "Are you going to let the doctors tell you when to die?"

Horrified, she looked at him saying, "As if I have a choice!?"

He continued calmly, "No…but God does. If you are meant to hold that grandbaby, you will be here to do it regardless of what the doctors say—and if you *aren't*—nothing they can do will keep you here…but either way, it is not up to them!"

Sarcastically she retorted, "Oh, you *believe* that!?"

"No. I *know* that. I've watched it play out too many times in my thirty-six years as a surgeon."

She shrugged and turned away, and he left, intending to come by again later…which he did, but she had already gone home.

Seven months later, he got a birth announcement in the mail with a blue cigar and a photograph of the woman holding her grandson and a note proclaiming, "You were right. He's beautiful!" A year later, he got another card with another photo of her blowing out candles on his first birthday, and then a year after that, a note from her daughter saying that she had passed the week before her son's second birthday of a heart attack. The pancreatic cancer never did take her.

The silence as he ended the story was broken by my soft but insistent "Okay…I get it…but I still would like to know the numbers… What are the statistics for my diagnosis?"

"Well, remember, they are only statistics…the real results are between you and God…and I think He has other plans for you." He then grudgingly revealed that the stage and cancer was more serious because of my age and its type. The "statistics" were grim. Eighty percent chance of recurrence in the first two years after surgery, and if it recurred, survival dropped to 20 percent for five years, less than 2 percent for ten. I felt my breath sharply intake with the words that finally opened the gates of full understanding, and exhaling loudly, I blurted out, "Well…*those* are shitty odds!"

For the first time, it really sank all the way in just how serious my situation was.

Gently, Dr. Armstrong chided, "Remember what I told you… It isn't up to statistics or even my surgical skill. *It is up to God*—and I think He has plans for you."

I responded with a soft "Yes" and hung up the phone.

For the first time, I was truly afraid. If it really *was* all up to *God*, I was in trouble. I wasn't even sure He cared, and I certainly had never really *connected* with this mysterious omnipresent God of the universe. I knew I needed to *pray*, but when I looked up, all I saw was ceiling, and to be honest, I was pretty sure my prayers weren't strong enough to penetrate!

I walked to the sliding glass doors, immediately deciding that I wasn't praying through glass either! I opened the door, and a salty damp ocean breeze slapped me to attention as I stepped onto the balcony.

The day was warm, sunny, and clear. Pelicans were gliding just above the wave crests and sea birds called from the shoreline as the incoming waves advanced and retreated to the rhythm of the ages. I looked up to the heavens where I imagined God was and began to pour out my heart.

"*God*…I don't even know if you hear me or are even there…and I am at a place where I cannot walk by 'faith' in what others have told me that you might exist or hear me…I need to *know*."

All of a sudden, all the angst and fear and confusion took over, and I began crying out from the deepest place of my being. I wept at the memories of all my mistakes and failings and begged for another chance to live rightly—asking for another *five years* to turn my life around. I was so young that I still thought *five years* was a *long* time. Tears streaming down my face, heart breaking, I looked up seeking answers from a God I hoped was there.

Looking up into the clear, blue sky, I watched in amazement as a full-scale rainbow stretched out in front of me (even in my unchurched state, I knew that the rainbow was a sign of covenant), but I was unprepared for what came next. I heard an audible interior voice telling me firmly, "In case you missed *that* one, here is *another!*" Watching incredulously as a second rainbow lined up beside the first like a giant M written across the heavens. I realized that I was witnessing a miracle. A sign of God's existence, a sign of His love for me, a sign *that He heard me*. In that moment I knew *God* was real, heaven was real, hell was real, and that everything was *okay*…no matter how it all turned out, whether I lived or died; it was all *good—because He was*.

All of a sudden, the fear was gone, replaced by a deep-seated *joy* that I had never experienced before. I was jubilant. *I wanted to celebrate!* I was dying, yet I had never *felt* more *alive* than in that moment. Years later, I discovered that rainbows never line up like that—they go over each other, or even in circles—but to this date, nearly forty years later, I have yet to see a photograph of what I saw that day.

Jubilant, I exploded from the front door of my friend's beach condo heading for the fancy restaurant across the street with the intention of celebrating my newfound freedom! I was met at the door by a tuxedoed maître d' and suddenly felt small and out of place. Looking at the menu, I realized the only thing that I could afford on the menu was the house salad, so I inquired if that would be acceptable. Towering above me, he nodded and smiled, saying quite kindly, "Of course, miss." At which point, I could contain myself no longer and cried out, "Good! Because I am *celebrating!*"

Mildly amused by my outburst, he inquired what it was that I was celebrating, and when I told him "Rainbows!" he lit up and exclaimed in a proper British accent: "Rainbows? *I love* rainbows! Tell me about your rainbows!" My story flowed out in a rush of excitement. Start to finish. When I said the "C" word, his face fell, but my joy was irrepressible and I cried out, "*No*…no sorrow—we are *celebrating* GOD'S GOODNESS *and* RAINBOWS!"

At which point, he again lit up and waving me to follow him into the dining room, declared, "*Then* CELEBRATE *you* SHALL!"

He seated me at a raised VIP table center stage, called the waiter over, and instructed him to bring me whatever I asked for "on the house." It was then that I realized my tuxedoed British gentleman was the owner, and my day had once again shifted. I ordered the cheapest item on the menu (chicken) and a glass of iced tea. My towering friend perused my order, sniffed, and shook his head, saying, "This will never do for a celebration." With a wave of his white, gloved hand, he instructed the waiter to bring what I'd ordered, along with surf and turf, baked Alaska, and a bottle of champagne! It was apparent God had moved again, and He was orchestrating an amazing over-the-top *feast* to celebrate! *I loved every moment of it.*

Chapter 7

Falling Deeper into Grace

My husband was through with reintegration and had been sent north for training in his new position. I moved in with my stepmom and began my new "job" of endeavoring to survive the cancer that had invaded my life. The whirlwind of appointments, bloodwork, X-rays, PET scans, and surgeries crowded my thoughts and my calendar. Overwhelming, it was a sheer tidal wave of one major/life/ death decision after another with no time for consideration or weighing options. It was now, now, *now*.

The first appointment (soon-to-be-weekly) bloodwork brought an unanticipated gift from an unforeseen source. The lady checking me in engaged me in conversation and, upon hearing my story, pressed a gift into my hand, saying, "I feel like God is telling me to give this to you. It is a rosary from Medjugorje." I had no idea what that meant, where Medjugorje was, or even how to use a rosary (though, I'd watched my mother pray it) but felt compelled to accept the gift humbly and carefully put it around my neck as a talisman to protect myself from what was yet to come. It was to become an important key into a new future.

Two days later, I was at the hospital for my first PET scan. Not knowing what to expect, I was surprised when they informed me (after injecting me with radioactive substances) that I would have to wait another hour before the scan could be done. Sitting in the waiting room surrounded by other cancer patients in various stages of illness and physical losses, I became anxious and decided that I still was not settled with God. I needed to see a priest. Perhaps there was one already *in* the hospital? I asked if I could walk around instead of sitting, and permission was given. I walked the halls looking for the sign of a priest's presence. Seeing the pastoral center on the floor below, I inquired if there was a priest in the hospital. The young lady behind the counter smiled warmly and offered to check for me. On calling the main office, she found that there were no priests scheduled to come in that day. As my face fell, she quickly came back with "Not to worry! There are *four* Catholic churches in the area! I am sure I can find you someone!" Picking up the phone, she began calling them one by one.

First church, no priest available, none that day. Second church, no priest available, none that day. Third church, no priest available, none that day. *Fourth* church, no priest available, none that day. She looked up at my stricken face, telling me not to cry, there was a pastor down the street that she was sure was available…and I stammered out between sobs, "You don't understand… I will talk to any man of God…but *what I really need* is a *priest!*"

Endeavoring to console me, she offered the little side room for me to wait in until I had to go up for my scan. There was a couch and a Bible. It was quiet and comfortable. I accepted gratefully. No sooner than I had entered and closed the door, an undeniable rage rose up in my spirit, and I angrily cried out to this *God* I had just come into relationship with—*I literally* YELLED at Him! Eyes full of tears, my broken heart raging, I bellowed, "WHAT KIND OF GOD puts someone in a religion that teaches them that they need a priest to return fully into communion with Him—and then THERE ARE NO PRIESTS?! WHAT KIND OF GOD DOES *THAT*?!"

That very second, the phone rang, and I heard the young woman's voice from the office say, "Yes, she is here! Send him right down!" I can still see the look on her bespectacled face as she opened the door and leaned from behind the door frame, exclaiming, "A *priest* just came into the hospital! He is on his way down!"

Now feeling humbled by my angry outburst, I was so overwhelmed by his unexpected appearance that I did not notice he looked a little pale and rather shaken. He was *big*. Well over six foot and a *large* man. I felt like GOD had entered, and in a very real way he *had*, though neither of us were fully aware of it yet.

I launched into my story, and midway through, he put on a stole, heard my confession, granted absolution, and offered me communion. Normally, that would have been denied me as I was not yet married in the Church (my husband still needed an annulment from his previous marriage), but the fact that I was now considered "terminal" gave him the opportunity to offer Christ's mercy in an unexpected way.

The moment was intense. The air around us rarified. It was as if everything was covered in liquid gold. Neither of us moved. Neither of us wanted the moment to end. We knew we were on holy ground. *JESUS was IN the room*. But I had to go. I had a PET scan to show up for. I broke the profound silence with my thank you, telling him what a Godsend he was. His reply was startling. "No. *You* don't know what a GOD-send I am!" Surprised, I looked up into his face, for the first time noticing his discomfiture, and asked him to elaborate, opening the door for a full explanation.

He let me know he was not from around here. He was a mission priest on assignment to a parish nearly forty miles away. He had come to a nearby mall to do some shopping, unexpectedly felt ill, decided to head back, took a wrong turn, missed the highway, and ended up in front of the hospital. Driving by, he heard an interior voice say, "Stop. Someone needs you." He immediately rejected the "thought," saying to himself, *That's ridiculous! I'm not even from around here!* and continued to move forward. He was then shocked by an audible voice firmly ordering "STOP! SOMEONE NEEDS YOU!" accompanied by a vision of an actual STOP sign dropping down in front of his vehicle! He hit his brakes hard. Set the car in Park and walked into the hospital door in front of him. To his left was the information desk, and they sent him to me! All of this had been set in motion *long* before I cried out to God in my anger and pain. *Months* before, as this particular northern priest was being assigned to give a mission in a southern town in the middle of nowhere USA. Before I had even received my diagnosis. Before we left the Rockies. Before

John joined the navy, before he was assigned to the wrong group. Perhaps all the way to when my husband humbled himself to give God his girl back three days after *the dream*.

In my lack of understanding, I thought I needed a priest to reconcile completely with God. Truth was, what we *both* needed was a face-to-face encounter with *Jesus* himself—and in *that* God-ordained moment, Jesus was undeniably in the room for the two of us.

Both of our life stories changed in that moment… but I am getting ahead of myself. You will have to *wait* for what Paul Harvey would refer to in my time glibly as "the rest of the story."

Chapter 8

A Pool of Mercy

I fell into a routine of seeing specialists, bloodwork, X-rays, tests, and subsequent surgeries. Surgeon. A modified radical mastectomy. Plastic surgeon. Expander. Oncologist. Chemo port. Six doses of FAC chemo. Plastic surgeon. Reconstruction. Port removal. I signed my left breast and a year of my life away—trusting in this GOD that had revealed Himself to me—as I entered into the whirlwind roller-coaster life of a cancer patient. My husband three States away, it was now GOD and *me*.

Tests run, go ahead given, I was checked in for surgery. Modified radical mastectomy. A big deal. I was too oblivious to be frightened and just willed myself to walk into the jaws of the bear. For the next six months, I would face down that maw over and over. This was just the first time of what would be many encounters. I did not know enough yet to be afraid. The procedure went well. It was the aftermath that hit hard.

In an unexpected grace, Dr. Armstrong admitted me to recover overnight before sending me home. This was when I found out that morphine was not my friend. The drip made me profoundly nauseous, and I found I preferred the pain to Madame Morphine's sickening grip. I still remember clearly the young blond nurse who came in to check on me; she noted immediately that I was suffering gravely and called for a change in pain meds. As we waited for the doctor to respond, she asked for permission to pray with me, which, with tears in my eyes, I welcomed by shaking my head an emphatic "yes." Not missing a beat, this tiny little spiritual powerhouse took me in her arms much as you would a small child, slowly rocked me back and forth and softly prayed over me. Though she was just a little thing, I felt small against her chest, and her heartbeat measured prayer brought relief and peace. With a deep sigh, I closed my eyes and fell asleep in those arms. I do not remember her laying me back down, and I never saw that kind face again… but her loving compassion and that sweet prayer are carried within the deepest part of me always. That nameless nurse opened doors within my soul of trust that needed opening. I needed to *know* that this GOD that had entered into my life with a sweeping set of rainbows, could address every issue that came up by sending his dear children to minister to me.

His love was a deep pool of mercy that called to me, cajoled me to jump in, and engulfed me in such waves of unconditional love that I entered fully into being swallowed up and totally immersed in this wondrous sea of love and mercy! I still did not understand this GOD that was showing up over and over, but I was beginning to understand the complete constancy of His love.

Dancing with Wolves

On returning home, the full extent of what my body had just endured at the hands of the surgeons became apparent. Pain was relentless the first three days, my bandaged chest pristine looking, hiding secrets that I was quite unprepared to see the third day during my first dressing change. I was swollen, bruised, and puckered. The large, stitched-up wound that crossed over the place my breast used to be, with fluid draining tubes attached to small bags, was a Frankenstein reminder that I would never be the same. I was horrified and, for the first time, glad that my husband was not there to witness the first casualties of this "war."

My initial visit to the oncologist came ten days later. The night before, I had a very intense, very real dream. It was so vivid that, to this day, I have not forgotten a single detail:

I was in a large meadow. I saw an interesting bohemian-type woman in a long dress walking toward an impressive mansion with large, regal dog statues on either side of the front entryway. I followed her, and she silently invited me in, signaling me to wait in the foyer as she disappeared into another room. The expansive foyer, made almost entirely of marble, had a raised circular area in the middle encased in a special glass etched with a giant compass. Under the glass were CLOCKS. Lots of clocks. Each labeled according to its purpose. *REAL TIME. PERCEIVED TIME. FUTURE TIME. PAST TIME. ACCEPTABLE TIME.* Some dials were moving slowly, some backward, some more quickly than one would expect. I could not quite make sense of it. Seeing a low, small fridge that appeared to be almost hiding in a corner, I went over to investigate and found the contents even more intriguing than the clocks. Several herbs with names I did not recognize, one labeled "Wormwood," and a package marked "Red River Wolf Meat." All of a sudden, I was aware that my mysterious lady had returned and was looking over my shoulder. Startled, I quickly stood up and apologized for looking through her things, and she calmly stated, "It is okay. This is important for you…especially the Red River wolf meat and the *timing*." Pointing back to the clocks, she declared, "*For you, TIMING is everything!*" Then I woke up.

Seeing the oncologist for the first time that morning, I carefully recounted the dream to her, watching her eyes intently to gauge her reaction. Watching her pupils narrow and widen, I held my breath, knowing my words had hit a mark within her and waited for her response. She admitted that she had been struggling with which course of action to take in my case, and my dream had given her the answer. The course of chemo she had been considering (called FAC) centered around the harsh drug called Adriamycin—nicknamed in her office by the nurses "Red River Wolf" as the patients would visualize a wolf coursing through their veins (the red river), hunting down all the cancer cells! The timing reference neither of us figured out until after the first dose of chemo knocked me down so hard, she went back and recalculated to make sure she had not overdosed me in error! The culprit turned out to be the flu shot she had given me the day before. On reading the literature, I found out the version that year compromised liver function for forty-eight hours. Since the chemo I was given was primarily metabolized by the liver—the poison just stayed in my system—relentlessly eating away at every dividing cell in my body. I threw up my intestinal lining, I lost muscle tissue in my forearms and the gut-wrenching nausea was nonstop for three days. Yes, TIMING was indeed EVERYTHING!

The Lady in the Mirror

Two weeks later, my husband was scheduled to come from his "A" school to visit me. It would be the first time that he had seen me post-mastectomy, and the concern that he would no longer find his girl attractive kept pinging my now fragile ego. He arrived on a Friday, and as I showered that evening in preparation for bed, the unthinkable happened. My *hair* fell out. *All of it*. All at once. A large clump of hair let loose into my hands, and another sodden mass lay at my feet in the drain. The shock of it was mind-numbing.

I knew my hair was going to fall out as a result of chemo. I had even cut my long locks short in anticipation…but I was not prepared for the all-at-once *thisness* of it.

I crawled out of the tub and looked into the mirror, not recognizing the woman that looked back at me. Her face was tight, dark circles under her eyes, sunken scarred chest, swollen left arm, bald with little patches and tufts of hair in a random pattern across her head! This was not *me*—no long-flowing mane of auburn hair, no shining eyes nor flashing smile. Body snaked with red raised Frankenstein scars, face pinched and darkened by the onslaught of the red river wolf coursing within her. I was paralyzed by the stark reality of this unfamiliar image in the mirror.

Hearing movement, I looked over to see the doorknob twist and realized my husband was entering and would see *this* "me" hairless…*vulnerable*…exposed. My heart fell into a tightening gut and my mind screamed as a dark pit opened in front of me. If I saw a look of horror, or even a hint of pity, I would be undone! The door opened. He stood there. In his eyes, there was no horror. No pity. Only *love* for his girl. His eyes shone with a tenderness I had only seen once before on our wedding day as we exchanged heartfelt "I dos."

Oh so tenderly, he gazed past all into my inmost being—seeing only *me*—the me that was *under* all the rest. The *me* that he loved… the *me* that loved him back!

We were going to be okay. *We were still* WE. The pit that had opened before me closed.

I did not fall in.

Chapter 9

Facing the Bear

That night we wrapped around each other the way that bodies that have become "one" do—despite all obstacles—finding new ways to hold, to connect and become whole again. We had four wonderful days together before he had to go back leaving me to face the bear again. Alone. My stepmom was still working and was too tied up and honestly too tired to be present, and I found myself creating a circular routine that hemmed my life in and kept me sane without my husband.

I *was* alone, and yet I was so wrapped up in GOD's love and care that I never once felt lonely. I would walk nearly a mile into town in an effort to strengthen my body against the onslaught of big-gun chemo and, in so doing, made many new friends along the way. A local art store gifted me with art supplies and gift certificates to the corner coffee shop. The thrift store next to them gave me "new" clothes and shoes to get me through the winter season, as I had come with a single suitcase not knowing that I would never again return to our little house in the Rocky Mountains. The teller at the bank brought in a winter coat, some sweaters, and a pair of walking shoes and surprised me with them when I came in to make a withdrawal from my account. The days I was too tired to walk back to my step-mother's condo, someone would close their store, put up a BE BACK SOON sign, and ferry me home.

I walked nearly every day in the glorious fall/early winter sunshine, endeavoring to strengthen my heart and body against the red river wolf's relentless attacks. I relished the feel of the cool breeze against my face, and the warm sun on my back and sang songs of joy as I made my way to and from. On the days my energy flagged, I would sing louder, and my steps would become more determined. Many a night was sleepless as my body screamed at me, complaining about the inflicted treatments—and those nights became cherished prayer times spent communing with this GOD I now knew existed and was learning to trust and love.

One night after a particularly difficult day, I found myself deep in conversation with my new beloved. I had walked into town enjoying the birds singing and joining my songs of praise with theirs but had found myself unable to make it back home again, sitting on a storefront stoop waiting for strength to return. A kind soul noticed and brought me home and I crawled into bed to recover, staying in my room for the rest of that day and into the night. The next morning was to be my third dose of chemo, and my body was already dreading it; sleep was impossible. In those wakeful moments, though, I found myself rejoicing, pondering all the blessings of the past months and the goodness of the LORD in my life. As I recalled His presence, I marveled at how HAPPY I was, and I exclaimed to Him aloud how amazing it was to be dying and yet be *so* unafraid and happy in the midst of it! Continuing in my exuberance, I declared, "In fact, PAPA"—I had begun to affectionately call Him my PAPA-GOD—"the only thing that I can think of that would make me any happier than I am right now in this moment, *is if...IF YOU CAME INTO EVERY CELL OF MY BODY!*"

With that declaration, white light poured over me from the corner of my little room. Glorious, white light. Living white LIGHT. Palpable, thick, shimmering GOD LOVE LIGHT! I sat embraced by its glow for what seemed to be a long time, not wanting to move. Finally, the light dissipated, and I was left in awe of what had just occurred.

GOD HAD BEEN THERE.

Where GOD had been so long and so completely, cancer could not stay. I was convinced that without my asking—I HAD BEEN HEALED—*I slept.*

In the morning I went into the oncologist's office to tell her I was done. No more chemo. The staff was shocked and gasped like fish abruptly pulled out of water, proclaiming, "You can't *do* that! You will die!" and immediately called for the doctor to come talk some sense back into me! She looked startled but listened to my story and, in the end, did not quite know what to do with what I had told her.

It was decided that we would do two of the three chemotherapy drugs, deleting the Adriamycin from the mix, and she ordered a MUGA scan for the next day to see how my heart was doing. I thought keeping the red river wolf out of the equation would make the treatment easier—but such was not the case! I got sicker than EVER! (Perhaps it was not a good idea to put more of any kind of chemo into a healed body!) The biggest surprise though was the result of the MUGA scan. I was in complete congestive heart failure from the Adriamycin. Had I taken that third dose, I probably would have died. Not only *had He healed me* of my cancer, but He had *protected me* from the chemotherapy that was destroying my heart! Even more remarkable, the follow-up MUGA scan two weeks later revealed a completely normal heart! *I had a new heart!*

You can imagine how exultant I was! I still had no breast. I still had no hair. I still felt weakened. I still faced expander pump-ups and discomfort, reconstructive surgery, and a myriad of follow-up tests and bloodwork; yet I was so FULL of JOY I thought my HEART would BURST!

The bear was still there, but he no longer had death's sharp teeth to savage me. He might jump me, bruise me, beat me up; but I would live!

I WOULD LIVE.

Chapter 10

Freedom

A trip back to the mountains to pick up my car brought newfound freedoms. Our little house had been evacuated, household goods put into storage, animals rehomed, our tenant had returned to her husband and was doing well in her own place. All our concerns had been alleviated. The only thing left to focus on was returning to my new place of residence and continuing to get well. The best part was, with my car, life was no longer a walk-around. I could now drive. Go to daily Mass. Visit whom I wished, whenever I wished.

The perimeters of my world widened, and a new routine developed as we entered into the Lenten season. John was still in A-school, and both of us threw ourselves into seeking God as we traversed toward the EASTER mysteries. I began going to daily Mass. My husband was befriended by a holy priest at his new naval base that had just returned from Medjugorje. This was the second time we had heard of that place of pilgrimage, but certainly would not be the last. GOD *had PLANS* of His own.

First Eucharistic Miracle

Part of the new routine was going to daily Mass. I liked the order of it, the sacredness of the space and the opportunity to set time apart to *be* in His presence, to listen for his voice. One cold winter morning, I came in expecting Mass and found something quite different happening. Everyone was kneeling quietly, some praying rosaries, some reading out of devotionals, and instead of a priest saying the Mass, the altar held a large golden "sun" with a white center, surrounded by candles.

I entered and followed suit, kneeling quietly and looking at the "sun" on the altar trying to figure out what exactly was happening. Someone coughed to the right of me, and I turned to look; noticing as I did, a profound warmth on the left side of my face. My first thought was that it must have been colder than I thought outside, but as I turned to face the front again, the warmth unexpectedly moved to the front of my face! I tested it by turning my face to the left, finding the warmth was now on the right side and in *that* moment realized where the warmth was emanating from! It was coming directly from the "sun" on the altar! The warmth felt "alive" pulsating with energy—the "sun" WAS THE SON! It was JESUS! I recognized that aliveness! I recognized that LIGHT! I was already on my knees, but in that moment, my SOUL dropped to its knees in adoration, and I was undone!

It seemed only minutes later that the priest appeared and was taking the SON away, and I literally cried out, "No! Don't take Him away!" The lady sitting to my left, looked over at me and said softly, "Honey, you've been here over an hour!" An hour is too short when you are sitting in the LIGHT. I was heartbroken. That is the first time I knew CHRIST was truly present, body, soul, divinity, in the Eucharist. It would not be the last.

LENT was incredibly sweet for both of us that year. Even though we were living apart, we walked it together. GOD was showing up for my husband through a holy priest's counsel, and I kept seeing GOD everywhere I looked! There were no cell phones and long-distance calls were expensive, so we wrote, letter after letter. Each night pouring out our hearts to one another on paper. Weekly missives showed up in our mailboxes to rekindle, encourage, and remind us whose we were.

Larissa Kay Ellis

The Second Eucharistic Miracle

The third Sunday of Lent is called "Rose Sunday." Entering the church just before Mass began, I was channeled to the front, where seats always seem to be open in a Catholic church, even when the back pews are full shoulder to shoulder! Second row in, I had an unobstructed view of the altar—which after today—would become my seat of preference in any church. That day, I found myself marveling at how much easier it was to see and focus on the Mass sitting front and center and how it was easy to "be" in God's presence. My head was covered with a silken cream scarf interwoven with intricate gold threading. My husband brought it home for me after my hair fell out as an impromptu gift—wrapping its soft silken glory around my scruffy bald head and declaring me his "beautiful, beautiful girl." His "love gift" made me *feel* beautiful, and I wore it out often, and to *every* Mass. This Mass was no exception. The music wound over and around the congregation, and I felt enveloped, almost as though I could feel heaven bending low, and the brush of angel wings…little did I know how *real* that feeling *was! All I knew was that I felt incredibly connected to everything that was happening…*

Midway through the Mass, the priest elevated a large host during the prayers of consecration and all of a sudden clear as DAY I saw an image of the face of the crucified JESUS on the nearly six-inch elevated Host—beaten, bloody, right eye swollen shut, angry thorns pressed into his scalp, blood dripping from his brow. I was stunned by the vision of this suffering, and as I gasped audibly, I heard a voice softly proclaim, "Oh, not for you!" and the vision disappeared as quickly as it had appeared!

The rest of the Mass swirled around the shock of the vision and its rapid disappearance with the cryptic "Oh, not for you!" I did not understand what had just happened nor why it was "not for me." For the rest of what ended up being a very long Sunday, I wrestled with what I saw and what it might have meant.

Monday morning found me on the priest's rectory steps early, hoping to catch Father before his day began in earnest. I was surprised to find that someone had beat me to the punch and was already in his office talking to him. As I waited, the vision replayed in my head and unanswered questions manifested. I watched a rather subdued gentleman leave the rectory and I was invited in. I clearly remember Father's warm welcoming smile and sitting in front of his large desk as he inquired gently: "How may I help you?"

The events of the previous day flew out of my mouth as my eyes scanned his searching for understanding and meaning. His demeanor immediately sobered, and his eyes held mine steadily as he quickly proclaimed, "I know why you saw what you saw and heard what you heard!" Startled, I begged him to explain.

The explanation turned out to be far simpler than I ever could have imagined. The man that had come in before me had been stunned during the elevation of the Host as well. He'd seen the same vision of Jesus I had—the only difference being—he had ASKED God to provide something to restore the faith that was dying within him! God in His generosity and love for this soul had acquiesced, and because I had been communing so intimately with heaven, the veil was thin over me, and I had seen too! Once the angels were alerted by my gasp that I was also seeing, I'd heard the "Oh, not for you!" and the vision had disappeared. Father knew that a true eucharistic miracle had occurred, substantiated by our matching stories, and I realized the feeling of angel wings and heaven touching earth before the Mass started had been more than a mere "feeling." The spiritual realm was becoming increasingly real! My soul felt such relief with this new understanding, and I left rejoicing!

I had never seen an image like the one that appeared before my eyes that morning, and the closest thing I have ever seen to it since, was the image Mel Gibson chose for his movie DVD cover for *The Passion of the Christ* that came out many years later. That was the Jesus I saw.

Nearly twenty years after the movie came out in 2004, Jim Caviezel stated in an interview that his daily prayer to God during the project filming was that people would "see Jesus, not him." I think his request was honored in ways he has yet to learn this side of heaven.

Chapter 11

Easter Mysteries

Every Mass became holy ground for me after that vision of Jesus on Rose Sunday. I entered into the readings, listened intently to the homilies and liturgical prayers of consecration, knowing that something very REAL was happening up there on that altar. Many Sundays I would become aware of angelic presence—not necessarily "seeing" with my eyes, but rather "knowing" in my spirit—hard to explain, but real nonetheless!

John came home for Easter; our reunion was transcendent. We had both connected hard with our spiritual selves over the forty days of Lent—and now it was as if we were connecting on all three levels of being now—physically, mentally, spiritually. The spiritual aspect seemed to elevate the other two and when we came together as man and wife the act itself was very different. It *felt* extraordinary…holy. It was so surprising to me that I actually talked to our priest about it. He told me that we were experiencing our union how it was originally gifted to us and designed to be. Talk about a mind-shift for a once totally secular woman!

Holy Week was just that for both of us. HOLY. Neither of us had ever experienced the TRIDUUM of Holy Thursday, Good Friday, and the Easter Vigil. The biblical story, played out in the symbolism and intense connection we felt those nights, ended with the sheer JOY of a spectacular sunrise Easter Sunday Mass on the beach. It was the first time I had ever heard the JESUS STORY told from beginning to end.

I was starting to understand. I was getting hungry for more. More information. More GOD. More JESUS.

John returned to A school, and my circle grew bigger to include daily Mass and a local charismatic prayer group that had no trouble embracing the visions and experiences I shared and welcoming me as a sister in Christ! Here I found an entire group of people that did not find my stories extraordinary—they were merely stories of a soul that was connected to their Heavenly Father—and I felt a belonging that I had not felt before. We prayed, we sang, we rejoiced together as we studied our Bibles and saw the Word open up in new ways inside of us.

I began to gain strength slowly but surely, and my hair began to come back, but instead of wavy auburn locks, it was snow white for half an inch, changing abruptly to a stark black as it continued to grow. But the biggest surprise was yet to appear. Curl. Kinky, tight curl. I'd never seen anyone take care of really curly hair, so I had NO idea what to do with it. I brushed it. BIG mistake. (Can you say Afro?) Yikes, black curly frizzy hair with white tips. My first visit to a hair salon got the white cut off and a quick lesson in curly hair care. I came home with soft lovely dark curls that framed my face and I dubbed the new addition my "angel hair." I decided to love it and embraced my new look and regime.

My relationship with this GOD I could not see developed in ways that I never could have foreseen pre-rainbow. I talked with Him often as I walked the beach shoreline, waves lapping at my feet, the sun's radiant fingers caressing my shoulders and back. Our conversations were intimate, and I basked in the attention of this loving presence I called PAPA. As I walked and listened to the ageless shoreline's symphonic rhythm, I began to hear Him internally. Not a voice per se but definitely HIM:

"See this ocean? My Mercy is BIGGER than this—it is unfathomable."

"Feel My love light shining on you!"

"See My creation! Rejoice in it!"

How I loved those days of being HIS completely…no other-worldly cares or familial demands to take my attention away from Him; they are still a most cherished memory. In a very real way, it was our "honeymoon" I guess! I felt singularly LOVED. Singularly HIS.

Chapter 12

All Things Made New

The prayer group became my family, and their leader, a spiritual mentor. She noticed the rosary I had been gifted by the receptionist around my neck and began to share with me about the part of the world it came from. Medjugorje was a place of miracles. A place where heaven was touching earth. Despite being in a communist country, Medjugorje was a place of pilgrimage and hope for millions. Thousands streamed there hoping to see visions or a miracle. I found the stories intriguing, but I had no desire to *go*. After all, I had already had my miracles, seen visions and needed no more proof of His existence! Little did I know that even then the next step of my spiritual journey into wholeness was being staged and set into place!

My body had recovered enough for the plastic surgeon to schedule my reconstruction, and the date was set. I was no longer silly enough to be ambivalent about surgery and asked the prayer group to gather in the church before the Tabernacle to pray for the surgeon's hands and decisions to be guided and all to go perfectly. They did just that, and their intercessions were answered in an undeniable way—the reconstructive surgery went *so* perfectly that when it was done, the surgeons (I had two) literally DANCED in the OR, rejoicing at the outcome!

The result was beautiful. I was no longer Frankenstein. I looked whole again. I could look in the mirror and SMILE at what I saw instead of cringing. My cancer journey was coming to an end. The bear had bitten, the wolves had devoured, but I had not been destroyed. I had fought the battles well, and in the end, GOD stepped in and won the war.

My story spread, and I was invited to give my hospital "priest off the street" testimony at a Rosary luncheon. I accepted, and as I stood to share my story, an odd thing happened. Midway through, a woman stood up in the middle of the room, interrupted me, and relayed the last half of my story. Totally shocked as I'd not told the story except to a few close friends, I asked her how *she* knew *my* story?! She exclaimed that *he* had been their mission priest, and that I had been the subject of the entire weekend's mission; how GOD still uses his priests to HEAL his people—and his PEOPLE to heal his priests! I had been right. GOD HAD HEALED US BOTH THAT DAY. And that revelation was what Paul Harvey in my day referred to as "The REST of the story!"

I have often wondered what happened to that priest, how his ministry changed after our encounter. I know how profoundly *my* life changed course after his detour to the hospital. He would be in his late nineties now if he were still alive. Perhaps he will be one of my "greeters" when I get to heaven's shores; I rather like that thought. If I see a six-foot-plus man standing in the crowd, I will know who he is even without his roman collar!

My husband finally completed his avionics training and was assigned to his new station up north on the East Coast. He headed south in his no longer new but trusty car, and together we made the journey to our new home. Initially, we stayed on base, but eventually we moved into a townhouse within the city limits. Rent was high for a junior enlisted sailor, and in order to make ends meet, we took on a roommate, which seemed to work out well. The Catholic Church was close by, and we began annulment proceedings for John so that our marriage could be blessed and ratified.

I was no longer in danger of dying, so I had to go back to "spiritual communion" rather than taking communion with the rest of the congregants until the Tribunal made their judgment on John's annulment. Luckily for me, GOD was not bound by the rules, and the spiritual communions were intense and sweet and far from being punishment—though I did miss the taste and physical presence of the host in my mouth.

It was during this time that we received a phone call. It was my spiritual mentor from my charismatic prayer group. She had tracked us down through military channels and was calling with a startling offer. She announced that she had my airline ticket to Medjugorje and that I was to go the week of Thanksgiving. I replied that it could not be *my* ticket as I had never signed up to go, nor was I interested in going. At which point, she came back with, "Oh, it definitely *is* your ticket, and I think you will not refuse once you hear the rest of what I have to say."

Apparently, with every arranged pilgrimage tour, there were two free tickets given—one for the accompanying priest and one to be given out at the discretion of the tour group leader. Both had been distributed. The young woman who had initially been given the ticket went immediately to the church to thank JESUS for the gift. Kneeling in front of the Tabernacle, she had actually heard an audible voice saying, "It is not your ticket. *It belongs to Larissa.*" She did not know a Larissa and came to my mentor asking if *she* might know who "Larissa" was. She did. My mentor was right. I had to reconsider. How do you refuse a free ticket from JESUS?! I saw no need to go. But I did not know how to gracefully say no to a $2,000 gift from JESUS and decided that perhaps, GOD knew something that I didn't. I acquiesced.

A week later, it became apparent that GOD was way ahead of me. A very good friend had asked me if I wanted a lovely (expensive) lace panty that did not fit her; and I took it home, tried it on, and told her yes as it was comfortable and so pretty! What she didn't know was that because she had tried them *on*, they were now carrying a viral surprise, and when I put them on, I became the recipient. Four days later, I had a horrible blistering rash that was diagnosed as genital herpes! I was HORRIFIED. Not POSSIBLE! Where or how could I possibly have been exposed?! I felt dirty, broken, and telling my husband was worse than telling him I had CANCER.

Crying into my friend's shoulder, I told her of this terrible turn of events and was shocked when she blushed red, her eyes wide, and blurted out that I had surely gotten them from HER...*via the PANTIES!* She had *no* idea that it could be spread that way. She was not in the middle of an outbreak...but there it was. The doctor told me it was a permanent affliction that would come and go as my immune system ebbed and waned and provided gel to help it heal. All of a sudden, I DID need to go to Medjugorje. I DID need a healing. I needed a MIRACLE.

Two days later, I was to leave for Medjugorje. My husband drove me to the airport in Baltimore and, on the way, decided to take a different route. It cost us nearly an hour, and by the time I ran breathless to the boarding gate, my plane was GONE. It had already pulled away from the gate and onto the tarmac. Bursting into tears, I desperately cried out to the gate attendant that I needed him to make it STOP! To wait for me! *It wasn't MY fault that I was late!* The words rolled out of my mouth in a torrent: *I HAD to be on that plane!* I was on my way to Medjugorje. I *HAD* to make the connecting flight in New York! I couldn't tell him about the herpes—but I told him that I had just finished chemo and that my HEALING was waiting for me in Medjugorje! *PLEASE, PLEASE, PLEASE!* He looked at this out-of-breath, frail, nearly bald, large-eyed panicked soul intently for the briefest of moments; picked up the phone, talking directly to the pilot, AND STOPPED THE PLANE ON THE TARMAC. They took me out across the black asphalt, pulled a rolling stairway for me to climb, and I GOT ON THE PLANE, luggage in hand. People stared, wondering who this person was that they would stop a PLANE for. Was she a movie star? Someone famous? No. It was just little me. THAT was the day I found out GOD can do ANYTHING for ANYONE—including stop a plane pre-9/11!

The flight from New York was long, with a short stop in London to refuel. I felt disconnected from the group. I did not know them, and they did not know me, and though they were kind enough, there was no real connection between us. We landed in Yugoslavia, a bus transported our group to Medjugorje, and once there, we were divided into welcoming homes. There were no hotels in those early days of pilgrimage there—only generous souls who were eager to share the gift of heaven touching Earth on their mountain! My host home was spartan but generous of spirit, and I felt welcome there. The group had arranged for various activities, and I attended them all. But it was my time alone on the hill of apparitions that made it clear why I had been called to this place.

The weather was cold and overcast, the way up the hill steep, rocky and somewhat tricky to navigate in my weakened state. I talked to myself as I climbed, "You can do this. Don't quit, keep on going!" I crested the summit and looked out over the valley below, all of a sudden deeply aware that this place was different—VERY different. It was as though HEAVEN itself were bending low, and if I raised my hand high—I could TOUCH it. I found a large rock and sat against it allowing this sense of heaven to enfold me and began to weep. I wept for my brokenness, for all my mistakes, for the great graces I'd received and for being blinded by the world. The longer I prayed, the lower heaven dipped until I was awash in its presence! A cold drizzling rain began to fall—but I was unwilling to move—I wanted to stay on that mountain forever! As I sat there, eyes closed, short chemo hair, thin bodied, shivering with cold, another pilgrim came up and covered me silently with his warm coat, allowing me to remain. He knew he would probably never see that coat again and yet he gave it freely, and I know GOD blessed him for it.

The next day, I stood in a line that wrapped around the block waiting for the Sacrament of Reconciliation watching people coming into the town by the thousands, some walking literally on their KNEES, rosaries in their hands, praying as they came! The air was sweet and sacred, and GOD was centerstage. My confession took a long time. I wanted to be thorough—I wanted no sin or failing to stand between me and this GOD who was now overwhelmingly PRESENT. He had come to my room the night of my healing, He had entered into me and *healed me* there—but THIS was different—BIGGER and well beyond explanation. My penance was to climb the Hill again, this time declaring with every STEP: "*I belong to CHRIST!*"

The day was hot, the sun unrelenting, but the ascent was easier than the first time and my heart soared with every step as it became written *in me*—I BELONG TO CHRIST! Something undefinable shifted within my soul and spirit. So much was happening within me, and yet if I had to put it all into words I could not.

The rest of the week was spent traversing through the village, climbing apparition hill and walking the stations of the cross, up the aptly named Cross Mountain. Our last two days would be spent in a small hamlet close by going to a healing Mass and then on to Dubrovnik. I continued to wrestle with the herpes infection, and the pain was a constant reminder that I was still in need of healing. I was certain that our journey to this church would bring that gift during the healing service. I just KNEW that was *why* I was here—why I had been given the ticket, and going to these places were pieces of the puzzle GOD was putting together within me.

The drive through the Yugoslavian mountains was indescribably beautiful with peaks and valleys, raging waters visible below us as the narrow roadway dropped off, steep cliffs slipping into an indigo sea. As we drove, storm clouds gathered, and an unexpected earthquake shook us as we disembarked. The rain came after we'd entered into the church, and as it pounded on the roof, I took in the magnificence of this not-so-little sanctuary in the middle of nowhere. To my left was the statue of Our Lady that was pictured everywhere in Medjugorje; but to my surprise, this statue was pale, almost white—nothing like the brightly colored pictures I had seen in town! I thought to myself even *pictures* of things cannot be trusted and wondered why they had colored them that way! Was it so they would sell more? My skepticism then astonishes me now.

Mass began, and at the close was to be the healing service I had anticipated and longed for. The liturgy ended, and those desiring healing were invited forward to receive prayer from the row of priests that had come forward to intercede for us. I made my way into the parish priest's line, *certain* that I was about to be healed; my heart was pounding, and I was expectant. Imagine my surprise when he passed over me, quickly making a brief sign of the cross on my forehead! I was devastated! I wanted to cry out, "No, no! Come BACK! You've made a mistake! I am supposed to be *healed* here!" Instead, I returned to my pew crushed, tears streaming down my face as I mourned the loss of my moment of healing. I looked up at the large bloody crucifix above the altar (they are not cleaned up images of Christ's passion like we see in the States), and I internally cried out to the JESUS I saw hanging there. I immediately became transfixed as I noted His eyes opening and His gaze meeting mine. Silently, I poured out my heart; I had done all I knew to do, gone to confession, climbed the hill and the mountain, repented, and prayed; why was I not healed? His gaze steady, eyes locking mine, I heard His voice clearly—an interior voice—savior to soul, soft and sad: "*YOU ARE NOT EVEN SORRY...*"

Shocked and hurt, I responded quickly, "How can you *say* that? I've done everything. I even went to confession *twice* to be sure I got it right!" At which point, His eyes closed, and his head lowered as he judged my heart in a hushed tone:

"*YOU HAVE BEEN SORRY BECAUSE YOU WERE HURT, SORRY BECAUSE OTH-ERS SUFFERED DUE TO YOUR FAILINGS, SORRY BECAUSE OF CONSEQUENCES. BUT NEVER ONCE HAVE YOU BEEN SORRY FOR WOUNDING ME.*"

The pain in His voice was clear. I had grieved Him gravely.

My heart dropped into my feet. He was right. Never once had I considered how my actions affected GOD or the KINGDOM. A wave of all-encompassing sorrow washed over me. For the first time, I experienced true contrition for my sins, and in THAT moment, I received my healing. A bolt of lightning struck close by, and the lights in the church went out.

It was the time of the apparition in Medjugorje, and we waited in the dimly lit sanctuary, praying silently rather than rushing to the awaiting bus. As I gazed up at the pale statue of Mary, a remarkable thing happened: Color began coming back into the statue beginning at her feet and ending with her face! Her eyes seemed alive and shining with tears as her face flushed with pleasure! She now was exactly as she was depicted in the pictures I had seen being sold in town. There was a distinct feeling of relief and JOY emanating from her that I did not yet understand. In fact, I wasn't even sure of *what* I was seeing. When I asked others if the statue had appeared pale to them or brighter colored after the lights went out, they just looked at me strangely and shook their heads. Needless to say, I kept my conversation with JESUS on the cross to myself, not wanting to be the weird one with the crazy story. It wasn't until I was seated on the plane to come home that all would become clear.

I sat alone on the bus, isolated by the surrealness of my experience. That night, in the quiet of my room, I replayed what I had seen over and over in my mind, as a nascent understanding began to be birthed in my spirit—not only was GOD present and choosing to love me, *He desired my acknowledgment of his love and suffering for me in return.* My lack of acknowledgment, not my sins, had been what had wounded Him most!

The blistering painful sores that had tormented me daily for my entire stay were not just better; they were GONE. If I had any doubts about what I had seen or not seen, my healing was indisputable. I had been made whole a second time by a GOD of mercies I did not yet fathom.

I was too stunned by what had occurred in that dimly lit sanctuary to enter into benign conversation with other house members, so I kept to myself at breakfast the next morning. The others assumed that I was worn out by all the travels and let me be. We left shortly after for Dubrovnik for afternoon Mass at the old cathedral in the city and an evening of exploration. We were sent to our rooms on arrival with instructions to return to the bus at four o'clock for transport to the cathedral. My roommate encouraged me to rest with the promise to wake me when it was time to leave. She did not. They left without me.

I woke up to an empty room, ran downstairs, and realized that I had been left behind. This was to be my first opportunity to receive Communion since JESUS had untangled the spiritual knots in my understanding of who He was and what He wanted from ME—and I was not about to miss it! Distressed, I enquired at the front desk how far it was to the cathedral, got very basic directions and began running. I would have to *run* to be in time for the Mass, and more than anything, I wanted *to be in the presence* of this JESUS again—to be in communion with Him! My body was still weakened from the ravages of my cancer journey, and I should not have been *able* to run the mile and a half to the church, but run I did—*the entire way*. When I became unsure of my bearings, an English-speaking soul (incredibly) was there to direct my path. I believe the angels assisted me that day. *There is no other valid explanation.*

I arrived in time. Everyone was shocked to see me walk in breathless, and even more surprised to learn that I had run all the way there rather than miss this encounter with JESUS. As an added bonus, I was given the privilege of reading the scriptures during the liturgy of the Word. How alive those words were as I read them aloud; they reverberated in my spirit and the great expanse of the church echoed with the power of them! That day is written in me forever.

Chapter 13

Back into the World

The air was crackling with excitement as our busload of pilgrims left for Dubrovnik Airport, and the energy only increased as we flowed into the airport almost as a single living breathing organism. Nearly overcome with the sheer joy of bringing home that which we had encountered on the holy ground we had walked, we literally glowed as a group. It wasn't until we were seated in the gate that we realized the stark contrast that was playing out in front of us. The attendants at the gate, and the rest of the populace in the seats were quiet and grim. Not a single smile, no light conversations, and definitely no laughter! We had forgotten during the delights of our pilgrimage that we were still in a communist country, and here, many miles away from the miracles of Medjugorje, there were only the sobering realities of a harsh godless government.

Our plane was delayed due to maintenance issues and finally replaced with a different one. We began to board, but four of us were held back. Our seat numbers did not exist on the new plane, and we were told we would have to purchase new tickets to board! As our group leaders verbally wrestled with those who were "in charge," an impasse was reached. We did not have funds to purchase new tickets, and they did not have facilities to house us if we were left behind.

Grimly, the gatekeepers talked among themselves, shaking their heads and gesturing as the clock ticked and the plane was delayed another hour. In the end, a phone call was made, and we were permitted to board. The entire charade was almost unbelievable—except for the fact it was very real! Once on the plane, we quickly took off and were finally on our way home. Little did we know at that point what that hour and a half delay would cost us.

Once in the air, I ended up chatting with the two young men behind me that had been detained with me for having "no seats on the plane." Bound by our mutual trial, we fast became friends, and I conversed easily with them both in ways I had not with the others of our group. I even shared with them the experience of JESUS on the cross and Our Lady's statue at the healing Mass. Wide-eyed, one of them exclaimed, "Oh my GOSH! You have GOT to read THIS!" and pulled out a little blue book entitled *OUR LADY'S PRIEST SONS* by Fr. Gobbi. Rapidly skimming through the table of contents, he found what he was looking for and passed the book to me to read. There in black and white was my miracle, word for word. The statue of Our Lady pale with concern at the state of a soul, and then flushing with pleasure when the soul turned to JESUS repentant and bathed in mercy! My pulse quickened, and my face warmed as I realized this was a confirmation of what I had seen. I still did not know why GOD had chosen these ways to speak to me, but I was glad beyond all telling that He *HAD*!

The rest of our journey across the ocean was spent in sharing our many personal stories of God's goodness, and we literally glowed with God-light as we relived our moments of glory. As we basked in those moments of remembrance, I was startled by an interior message. I heard the command, "PRAY. NOW." I went to our group leader and told her what I had heard, and the urgency of the command. She laughed and said dismissively, "Don't be silly! I have been leading these tours for years, and we have never had an issue." I went back to my seat, told my new friends behind me about the voice I had heard, and the four of us started praying a rosary aloud softly.

Moments after we began, the plane shuddered mightily and dropped several thousand feet, launching anyone who was not securely buckled in, out of their seat! Suddenly, the entire cabin, fore and aft, was praying aloud with us as the captain came on over the intercom to tell us what was going on. We had flown into a storm and the turbulence would continue as we could not get above it. We were being diverted from London to the Dublin airport as the fog was too thick to land, and London airport had been closed. What we did not know was that the Dublin airport would also be closed by the time we got there, and no more planes would be permitted to land. The consequences of our delay in Dubrovnik were beginning to manifest.

Once in the airspace over Dublin, our plane began to circle, our pilot telling us that we were in a temporary holding pattern, waiting for permission to land. Truth was that we did not have the fuel to make it to another airport, and they were circling hoping against hope we might be able to land before the fuel ran out. What the pilot *did not tell us* was that they would need to use up the excess fuel in case no runway opportunity occurred, which would then force a dangerous open-sea landing.

What we DID know was that the plane was being buffeted by the storm and that it was definitely TIME TO PRAY. HARD. About thirty minutes in, the pilot's voice came over the intercom, strained but sounding confident, "A hole has opened up in the clouds right over the runway, and we are going for it. The drop will be immediate and steep, so hold on, and know that the loss of altitude is intentional." Our prayers intensified as the plane literally dropped out of the sky in a way I have never experienced before or since; we slammed onto the runway and bounced twice before the tires gripped the tarmac and we felt the brakes, hearing the engines whine as they tried to slow us before we ran out of runway!

We taxied to the gate with a corporate sigh of relief thanking God that we were safely on the ground, but it was not until I saw the pilot's ashen face and wide eyes that I realized that the command to PRAY NOW had been heaven-sent, and our safe landing through that opportune "hole" in the storm was heaven's response to our prayers! Yet another protective miracle.

Instead of a refueling stop, the weather dictated an overnight stay in Ireland; being of Irish heritage, I was delighted by the delay and committed to enjoying every moment! We were bused to the airport hotel still on a high from the successful landing, and most of us talked well into the night, including a young man that had been wrestling with what he had experienced in Medjugorje. He was roomed with two others who knew the tour priest well, and the four of them ended up talking all night long. God completed the work that had begun in the hills of Medjugorje in his resistant soul. The unexpected diversion and unspoken crash scenario had forced him to look harder at what had been revealed in Medjugorje and decide either for or against GOD. Looking death in the face tends to make the "fence" we think we are sitting on disappear!

His mother had brought him to Medjugorje, hoping for a miracle to restore this son to her after godless years of drugs and heavy-metal music had stolen him from the family, and a week there had not quite been enough. I believe our stopover in Dublin was just for him, and the young man that exited the plane the night before was not the same shining faced young man that reboarded the next morning! After take-off, he recounted his story (now testimony) to us and declared the change in his spirit permanent. He shone so brightly that no one doubted.

His mother got the miracle she prayed so long and hard for.

The energy aboard the plane was palpable; we had been preserved for a reason, and there was a distinct excitement surrounding all of us. I, for one, felt radiant! I had not wanted to come. I did not think I needed to come. I'd thought I had GOD all figured out (after all, He *had* healed me!) and that my life's path had been made straight enough.

How could I have been so mistaken?

How could I not know His Heart's longing for true contrition?

I knew He was the Savior—that He had died for us—but I did not understand the depth of HIS LOVE for me or what true contrition was. The heart-to-heart connection was not complete. Only the new-to-me understanding that HE WAS, that GOD WAS, IS, AND EVER SHALL BE. This trip to a place halfway around the world had changed everything. For the first time, I could see Satan's smokescreen, the deception and the lies. All I know is that I came back a different woman. Made NEW. No longer afraid of anything and wanting nothing more than to serve this GOD that had revealed Himself to me so unabashedly! Over the previous years I had come to believe that GOD was real, but now I believed IN HIM...in what HE could do IN me!

Chapter 14

Make Me Holy, Lord!

John picked me up at BWI airport angry and frustrated. Traffic had been difficult, and my plane was a day late; he was NOT a happy man! I, in contrast, was jubilant! I was bubbling over with joy and the desire to convey all the wonderful things I had learned about this GOD of ours during my encounters with Him in Yugoslavia. We were like oil and water.

I had begun receiving communion in Medjugorje after my experience with JESUS on the cross and was not willing to give up this heavenly food again. John could see (and feel) the changes in me but struggled with the realities of what my choices would bring to our marriage. If I choose to keep receiving Eucharist, we could not sleep together as man and wife until his annulment went through, and our marriage was blessed in the Church. Initially he rebelled against the idea of the Church having "rights" over him and his marriage bed and issued the angry demand for me to choose: *GOD or HIM.*

The challenge was an arrow to my heart for I knew that there was no choice. *GOD was in FIRST PLACE now,* and I was not willing to ever put Him in second place again. Eyes full of tears, I softly replied, "Oh, baby! Do not make your girl choose! *You will LOSE!*" The shock on his face was irrefutable; he had been *so* sure of my great love for him that my unwillingness to choose *HIM* over this supposed God entity was a genuine surprise!

Years later, he revealed to me *THAT* had been the first time he *KNEW* God was *REAL*. He knew I would never have chosen an imaginary God over my sure love for him. That moment of realization opened a new door of conversation for us. We both agreed that the first years of our time together were "out of order" and that, perhaps, a sacrificial offering of this magnitude could be offered in reparation and used by God to heal any spiritual damage that had been wrought unintentionally in our ignorance.

We prayed about it together and by morning, our decision was locked in. *We were going to offer GOD a gift of LOVE and REPARATION for all the years we had not loved*—for all the selfish fleshly living we had chosen instead of serving Him. Not because the Church said so, but because our HEARTS *wanted* to! Our priest was somewhat surprised by our unconventional decision to live as "brother and sister" until John's annulment came through so I could continue to receive communion, but he was willing to support us in our offering. We were entering in to yet another LENT together, and this one promised to be the most intense ever—and did NOT disappoint!

To assist us in our commitment to one another and to God, we developed a new way of intimacy that did not break our pact but allowed us to show love and affection for each other in a physical manner. We labeled them NSEs, near-sexual encounters. A neck nuzzle, a shoulder rub, a cradling against a chest, listening to the other's heartbeat, became special moments of grace, binding us together in ways we never could have fathomed. Our life together was being recreated. I had returned from Medjugorje profoundly changed. The biggest change being my relationship with GOD. He was no longer "out there" and separate but a PART of who I was, who I AM, which in turn would affect who *WE* were. What our "*us*" would now look like! It required shifts on both of our parts and the transitions were not easy ones.

LENT was the perfect timing for such a large project, and again, it felt as though GOD was way ahead of us in the planning department as the pieces fell into place. We were making spiritual progress together for the first time, and it felt good! What we thought would be this hard, difficult sacrificial offering was so much easier than we'd ever envisioned, and blessing after blessing fell on us as we journeyed through the forty days of Lent. Imagine our surprise when, just before Easter, our priest came to us and disclosed that John's annulment had gone through more quickly than anticipated, and he could now be welcomed into the church and our marriage blessed so that we could celebrate Easter together officially—on ALL levels—mentally, spiritually, AND physically!

We were exultant! I had already experienced what I had perceived as a "honeymoon" period with God, and this new territory I began to call my "over the moon" period. I was over-the-moon happy and over-the-moon in love. I wanted to be *HOLY*. I wanted to *be* His. So one night, laying in my bed alone while John was away on deployment, I asked for that; I asked God to make me HOLY.

Don't ever DO that.

Just as I had NO idea of how much I needed to go to Medjugorje and how far off track I still was spiritually; I had NO idea of what it would entail to become "HOLY." If I had realized just how much inside still needed healing, restoring, and changing, I'd never have asked to be put on the fast track. But I didn't...and I did. It took less than six months for me to take it back and cry "Uncle," but once again, I am getting ahead of myself...

Chapter 15

Walking into the Furnace

A phone call from my father just after Christmas cast a dark shadow over our lives as once again cancer entered into the picture. First my mom, then me, now my father. He had gone into the hospital with pneumonia and had been discharged with a new diagnosis—lung cancer. The military responded compassionately, giving John TAD orders so we could be present for my father in his final weeks. Like my mother before him, the journey was a mere six weeks from diagnosis to last breath. He chose to fight with chemo and radiation, and while it weakened him terribly and rendered him housebound quickly, the end result was the same. To the day.

His death was not like my mother's. There was no peaceful moment of Christ entering the room. Rather, it was a night of desperation, pain, and crying out for my husband (the strongest person in the room) to pull him up out of the grasp of that which seemed to be pulling him down. I continued to pray for my father's soul, asking God's mercy, hoping (hope against hope) that he and GOD were having conversation in these last moments of his struggle! So many Divine Mercy chaplets had been prayed for him toward this moment. Suddenly, he quieted, leaned back into the recliner's embrace, and let go. Tears began to stream down his face as he looked intently at something none of us were able to see. Minutes later, he breathed his last. My father was gone.

I mourned his death harder because I did not know if he ever connected one on one with JESUS. I did not know whether or not in those final moments he had accepted His friendship. Or if he realized it was HIS strong arm that he needed to "pull him up" out of the darkness that was closing in on him, not John's. In so many ways he *HAD* been a good man, and in the end, a really *GOOD* dad. I had learned to understand, forgive, love, trust, and enjoy him in ways I had not been able to as a child. His new moniker: Poppa-bear (much more Poppa than bear) spoke of my growing trust and affection. More than anything, I wanted to know that I would see him again on heaven's shore. There is an old Irish saying that it is a long way from the horse to the ground, and I was hopeful that in that space between life and dying my Poppa had discovered something integral about our Savior.

I really *was* an orphan then. I poured myself into my marriage and into my church life, and God provided me with a mother figure to see me through. She had embraced us as family during her marriage to my dad and continued to umbrella over us after his passing. We were separated by distance, but heartstrings kept us connected.

Thanksgiving was going to be special for us that year. I was healed, our marriage was healed, and life was GOOD. We felt singularly blessed. Physically, I was strong again. We rode our bikes in the summer heat on thirty-mile treks through the countryside, reveling in our youth and resilience. It was a happy time for both of us. John was flying on deployment eighteen days of every month, and I was busy going to church, praying, and loving life. At the end of each deployment, his return was a time of celebration for both of us. LIFE WAS GOOD.

The week before our second Thanksgiving, I found out one of my brothers was living in his car on the streets. Looking at each other and the blessings that surrounded us, the answer to the question that was never asked was to call him and tell him to COME. That was the battle line we never saw, drawn in the sand we did not know existed, for a war we were being thrust into. We were totally unprepared for what was coming. My prayer to be made Holy was being answered in an unprecedented way—my brother was to be the refining fire.

He arrived five days later, driving up in a huge boat of a car and we welcomed him in with open arms and hearts. What we didn't know was that my brother was homeless for more than one reason. He was not just having a run of bad luck after an on-the-job injury. Although he could appear quite normal for short spans of time, it quickly became apparent my brother was mentally ill. His eventual diagnosis was under multiple titles: paranoid schizophrenia, manic depressive, posttraumatic stress, as well as an obsessive-compulsive disorder. The problems began to manifest almost immediately. The furnace door opened.

There were so many issues. He was in constant pain. He did not sleep. Lack of sleep increased his mania. His embedded hatred of doctors and his old employers and what they had done to him spewed forth like a poisoned stream wrapping around his spirit. He drank a LOT of coffee. So much so that we thought perhaps decaf would be beneficial (a thought he rejected), so later, we attempted to add it into his regime by subterfuge. We bought instant decaf and mixed it with his regular Nescafe, thinking he would not notice and that it might help. It was obvious we knew little about paranoid schizophrenia or obsessive-compulsive disorder! OF COURSE, HE NOTICED. Only he did not let *us* know he noticed. It was at that point he became convinced we were trying to poison him. But I am getting ahead of myself here.

While John was deployed, my life became a whirlwind of doctor's appointments for all the issues my brother faced. He needed eye surgery. There were a myriad of tests to be run to try and track down the constant nerve pain that tormented his days and made for so many sleepless nights. The difficulties of dealing with his paranoid episodes became compounded by the fact that I was not feeling well.

I had been bitten by a tick that spring. Six weeks later, I was experiencing neck pain, headaches, night sweats, deep fatigue, and a sense that *SOMETHING* was very wrong. A visit to the military doctor assigned to me was not helpful. He refused antibiotics as my Lyme's test had come back negative. (That was before doctors knew that there were false negatives and were encouraged to treat according to history and symptoms.) I continued to get sicker and sicker.

My hip joints hurt so badly I could barely walk. My fatigue was so severe that a drive to the grocery store would leave me sobbing at the wheel, unable to garner the strength to get out of the car and go in to shop. I would just wait, rest, and drive back home feeling helpless in this body that was failing me without explanation. My husband was gone, my brother was unsympathetic and demanding, and I became enraged at the unfairness of it. I had given so much of my time and energy to his needs, and there was none left over for me.

The night before my birthday, I finally hit my breaking point. I exploded. My words were hateful and angry with a laundry list of hurts as I drove myself into my room with a slamming door as the exclamation point! I did not sleep that night. It was as though I could "hear" my brother's thoughts, and they were constant, ugly, and mean-spirited. The only thing that silenced the voices was to pray out loud. So I did. Until 3:00 a.m. Much later, I would learn what those "voices" actually were and where they were coming from.

At three o'clock in the morning, exhausted by our argument and the "battle of the voices," I realized how *very* sick I was. If I did not get up and take myself to the emergency room then, by the next day, I would be too weak to make it. Upon my arrival in the ER suite, the doctor listened attentively, discerned I had atypical Lyme, and proceeded to treat me accordingly. My response to the medication was diagnostic in itself; I immediately got SICKER, a classic rebound effect called a Jarisch-Herxheimer reaction, and over the next twenty-four hours, I developed shaking chills, fever, and a rapidly appearing rash. All of which disappeared again within hours of their appearance. Lyme disease was the unseen enemy that had been destroying me from the inside out. Unfortunately, the battle was now systemic, and a single course of antibiotics was not a cure, only a starting point. It would take me years to get this particular monster under control.

That horrible night with my brother was the beginning of a slow long downward spiral into the darkness he unknowingly carried with him. My husband, gone eighteen days of every month, left me alone to navigate the totally unfamiliar waters of paranoid schizophrenia, manic-depressive states, and posttraumatic stress distilled from the harsh discipline received at the hands of my father as the unfavored son. To say that I was unprepared for what was to come is a *HUGE* understatement. I fell short in so many areas. While I never failed to *love* my brother, or walk in forgiveness, my patience, my emotional reserves, and my temper too often fell short, and we both suffered because of it.

It was during this time that I actually cried, "Uncle!" Told GOD that I took it all back; I no longer wanted to be "a saint"! It was just too hard! In retrospect, I don't think He *stopped* the process as I asked, but He did slow it down so I could catch up!

I was still feeling broken and fragile several weeks later while ferrying my brother to another doctor's appointment forty minutes away. My husband was home; we were running late, already stressed by financial issues that had come up, and I drove straight into a speed trap courtesy of the state police. It was the final straw that broke this camel's back, and I came undone. The crack in my veneer was separating; fracture was imminent. I was breaking.

As the officer walked up to our car, I could feel the pieces begin to come apart inside of me, and I held my breath, silently crying out to a GOD that seemed distant in that moment. I believe now that the first policeman that came to my car was a godly man. He had a discerning spirit and, noting what was happening inside of this stranger in front of him, immediately gentled and offered to give me a warning rather than the ticket we deserved but could not afford to pay. As we sat waiting, the other officer came over and presented me with a ticket *he* had written. When I tried to explain that we were to be given a warning, he coldly stated (as he ripped it emphatically from his pad) the ticket was written and *that* was the end of story.

I burst into tears, a shroud of darkness settling over me, shutting my heart down as the pieces inside shattered and fell like broken glass within me. I was inconsolable. John assured me it would be okay. The tears stopped, but internally, I continued to mourn, knowing that our first Valentine's Day dinner together since he had rejoined the military had just been canceled. The money now had to remain in the bank to cover the ticket. I stayed distraught for the remainder of the morning.

Silently considering the loss of our date night in the car as I drove, then sitting shaken beside my husband while waiting for my brother to finish his appointment, I felt broken. There were no more reserves to draw upon. Life was asking too much, and I was unable to pass muster. I felt hollowed out and empty. Though the drive home passed through glorious countryside I saw nothing but my own brokenness and failures. I had lost touch with my GOD center.

I walked desolately into our house to find the phone ringing insistently, demanding to be answered. Imagine my surprise when I found out the caller was the police officer that had spoken to me initially and promised the warning rather than a ticket. He was calling to give us a Valentine's Day present. He asked if I had the ticket available (I did; it was in my purse) and instructed me to tear it up and throw it away as he had done everything necessary to render it null and void. His voice became gentle as he apologized for the other officer's behavior and wished my husband and I a blessed Valentine's Day! Truly, GOD had moved through this soul to minister to mine.

I hung up the phone, endeavoring to process what had occurred and realized that once again I had been rescued. I was slowly learning what a good, GOOD Father we have. He allows adversity to challenge his children to grow and gain strength and build character yet stops short when we are in danger of breaking in order to comfort and restore before stretching us again. Needless to say, that Valentine's Day gift from the officer and the resulting celebratory dinner out became signs of GOD's goodness to us both.

The testing continued, and though I often fell short, other times I succeeded in loving and standing in grace. GOD offered a respite from the lesson plan (as we were being assigned to a new station down south) by opening a place for my brother in a rehabilitation center. He would stay there; we would head south…alone.

It was a break we both needed.

GOD is good.

Chapter 16

____

New Beginnings

The move was a relatively easy one. Every step went smoothly, including finding the perfect, tiny, three-bedroom rental house well within our price range. Once again, GOD was preparing us for a future only He could see. I had no idea, but my daughter was going through a very difficult time with her dad over a boy and was about to come live with us. Seven years had passed since my divorce from her father. She, of course, had regular visits, but coming to live with us had never been discussed or considered. This was an unexpected but very welcomed turn of events!

Her restoration to my care granted me the opportunity to share this God I had learned to trust and love, and her little heart was like a sponge soaking up His goodness. She blossomed under the umbrella of this God-light, and many an evening was spent sitting on her bed talking about this new shared love of ours. Even though many teens have difficulty connecting with their parents during their teen years, she and I connected in such a way that we were able to step over the obstacles that would trip others up.

She had barely settled in when we got the call from my brother. He was checking out of the rehab program saying they couldn't help him, with the intention of coming to live with us again. All three bedrooms were now occupied, and in these early days there was relative PEACE. My daughter's young, cheerful presence was a good buffer, and conflicts in our little house were few.

Just before the lease was up on our tiny safe haven, John came home excited and breathless from a bike ride, saying he'd found our next house! We packed up into the car and drove five blocks over, four blocks down to find a four bedroom soon to be home, tucked under the trees waiting to embrace us! I should have known by now that the extra bedroom within was a foreshadowing, but I was still blissfully unaware, and delighted by the larger home and yard.

Once the move was made, it quickly became apparent that my brother would never be able to work again, forcing us to step into rescue mode, helping him to apply for Social Security disability benefits and arranging for Social Security disability lawyers to file when those claims failed. We found a good pro-bono lawyer, and they arranged the doctor's appointments and psychiatric exams that were needed to complete the filing successfully.

I will never forget the day I took my brother in to see the psychiatrist. The elderly doctor came out alone after spending over an hour trying to determine a diagnosis for his issues. He faced me with tears in his eyes, shaking his head, telling me that I had no idea what I was getting myself into. My brother was in all probability incapable of gratitude or love, and that we could not fix what was broken by taking him in. I was sure he was wrong. I was sure God was bigger than all my brother's problems. I was sure that I could love him through this.

I was wrong on all counts. So was the doctor. But not in the ways you would think. Had I known that we were saying "yes" to a twenty-year epic journey through a valley of fire—I probably would have bailed. I would not have asked that of my husband. There was no way for us to know how this self-appointed adventure of ours was going to play out, and we stepped into the fire together unaware that we were sorely unprepared for the battles that would confront us! What I did not see in the moment was how God was training us, shaping us through the challenges we experienced with my brother. I am certain that I would be a very different woman had we not given our "yes" to the journey!

Self-perception is a funny thing. In some ways, we are self-disparaging, holding ourselves to a yardstick that we can never measure up to, and in others, we are completely blind to the failings that we see mirrored so clearly in the people around us, waving our yardsticks with frustrated cries of "*I cannot believe they do not see this!*" All the while, missing the same faults in ourselves. My brother's presence in our lives ensured that I would begin to see what I was "missing." The saying, "When you point your finger at someone else, there are three fingers pointing back at you" has always made me cringe a little. I had come a long way over the past five years, but this girl still had a very long way to go.

God continued to intersect in our lives and shortly after our move led us to our new church home. Another bike ride led to the discovery of a Catholic church less than a mile away, and a last-minute visit dropped us into the middle of a group rosary prayer that pulled us in and made us welcome. Their priest was warm, welcoming and deeply charismatic. He was a big man. Gregarious, open, and not afraid to love and be loved.

Once a month he hosted a healing service, and it was during one of the services that I had my first shared vision of Jesus in that sanctuary. One of the prayer leaders was praying over and with me for healing, and as he prayed aloud, the most amazing thing happened. My head was bowed, my eyes were closed, yet I had a clear vision of dancing with Jesus, and as we danced, we circled higher and higher in a spiral toward the heavens. I saw Him gazing into my face; I was lean and slight in his arms. I felt my hair swish as He turned me, to the sound of a music that played within us both. The exquisite delight of being in my Savior's arms was totally indescribable. A sudden stop in the prayer being prayed over me brought me quickly back into the present moment. In surprise, I opened my eyes to find the man looking up then back down at me softly, affirming, "Yes, you and Jesus, dancing…I saw it too!" I had my answer. Jesus was still holding me close. I was still safe in His arms.

I was in the right place. I now had my home base for the eighteen days of every month that John would be absent. This parish would become mother, father, family to me. It was the first time I lived in community long enough to see the good, the bad and the ugly, to learn the lesson that God was IN the Church—*but the church was not* GOD—and I could not judge his children (or his Church) on the basis of one or two bad actors. It was *here* that I learned unconditional forgiveness. When deeply wounded by a fellow parishioner, I struggled with a lack of understanding and feeling of betrayal. I knew I had to forgive, so with great effort I held it all up to Jesus and tried to let go. We made peace with each other. Yet every time I saw this person in church the wound reopened, and it was many months before the sight of them did not elicit pain.

Part of the process for me was avoidance. I just stayed out of their path. One Sunday, as I bent my head in prayer after just such a moment, GOD spoke to me internally.

"So…I see… That is how it is… You want to live at the edge of heaven."

"Oh no, LORD! I want to be with YOU at the foot of your THRONE!"

Gently, the response flooded over my heart: "*You are forgiven AS you forgive. You have forgiven but carefully keep them out of reach, and so it must be with you and Me then.*"

The reality of the statement shocked me to my very core!

"Then teach me to forgive as YOU forgive, LORD—as far as the east is from the west—to embrace them so as to be ONE with YOU!"

As I walked out of the sanctuary into the foyer, there was my stumbling block; the words of rebuke still ringing in my ears, I rushed forward to greet them with a clean spirit for the first time since the incident occurred. I was finally FREE.

It was in this church that I felt His presence in new, deeper, even more profound ways during the Mass. GOD began to "school me" on what was actually happening when we gathered on Sundays to celebrate Eucharist. It was here that I again began to experience "seeing" angels, have visions, and grow in spiritual understanding.

One Sunday, I looked up as Mass began, and a giant rustic stone urn just appeared above and to the left of the altar. It tipped slowly, pouring a thick golden liquid light out over the congregation that waved and shimmered just over our heads like a glorious thick blanket of glimmering see-through gold! No one else seemed to be aware of it, and I rose up in spirit to meet it, seeing myself break through with a glorious splash of JOY, permitted for a moment to *be* in that space above. Then, it just as suddenly disappeared, and I was fully back in the actual moment singing the gathering song.

I didn't quite know what to do with what I had seen or who to tell. I documented it and shared it with my priest, but I don't think he knew what to do with it either and quickly dismissed it. Why was I permitted in the above space? Was everyone invited into those living waters? Are they shimmering over us at EVERY Mass? So many unanswered questions and no one that I could go to and ask!

These were still the days of unlocked churches, and there were many a night I would be in the sanctuary in front of the Tabernacle praying during the night watch while my husband was on deployment. I loved those nights at His altar in the presence of Jesus. I believe one of those "night watches" saved my husband's life, or at the very least prevented serious harm.

I had been at home preparing to go to bed when I was overcome *with the urge to go to church and PRAY for my husband.* I had learned not to ignore these promptings. I immediately made the short trip to the church and went in to pray. I stayed nearly two hours. It was well after 1:00 a.m. before I headed for home. I had just showered and gotten into bed when the phone rang. It was two in the morning, my husband had obviously been drinking, and soon it became equally obvious that my prayer time had *mattered.*

As his story unwound, the safety net that had been cast around my husband became apparent. The crew had gone to Duval Street in New Orleans, and over the course of the evening the group had broken up, and my husband had gone his separate way, even though doing so would mean walking home alone. Unfamiliar with the streets of New Orleans and drunk enough to be fearless as he skipped along singing the "Our Father" (telling me later it was the only song that came to mind), which is doubly odd, as he is a heavy rock fan and *never* sings. Not even in private. He naively crossed into a dark neighborhood that stood between him and the bright streets of the hotel in which he was staying. The street was lined with drug addicts, pimps, and prostitutes; and he was in the path of direct contact, late at night, with no policemen in sight. All of a sudden, a large buxom black woman appeared mysteriously out of nowhere on the opposite side of the street, yelling, "*YOU! White boy! Yes, YOU! Get your white ass over here and listen to me!*"

She was hard-edged, plain-spoken, and deadly serious. I believe GOD sent her in response to my impromptu midnight vigil on my knees interceding for my husband. He crossed the street and stood before her. It was glaringly apparent that he did not belong there or understand the danger he was in.

"*Now you listen to ME, white boy—an' you listen GOOD if you want to make it back to your hotel alive tonight!*" Asking where he was staying, she gave him directions and instructed him to walk on the side of the street they were on only, to make eye contact with no one, to speak to no one, and to walk deliberately without stopping. Definitely *no* singing or skipping! Her attitude and warning were sobering, and following her instructions, he made his way back to the hotel without incident. New Orleans could be a dangerous place for the uninitiated, and my husband found himself grateful for a praying wife and the guardian that had come out of nowhere to rescue him! I shudder to think what might have happened if our black angel had not been sent that night on her assignment to assist my husband or if she had decided to ignore the prompting and stay home instead!

My second midnight call to pray for my husband was another protective net thrown over him during a trip to England. The crew had ridden the Tubes all through London ending up in a little SOHO district pub. The longer they were there the more uncomfortable my husband became. On the street, there had been advertisements for a peep show in the basement club below, and the rest of the crew decided to see what it was about. I had given my husband a scapular (a sacramental) to wear while he was gone. It had become very uncomfortable in SOHO, feeling almost like it was burning his neck. The discomfort kept him focused on me and God, so he had no desire to follow his fellow crew members downstairs and decided to wait for them in the pub above.

Within the hour, the crew rushed back up the stairwell, white-faced and shaken! It had been the classic bait and switch set up, and once down there, the drapes were pulled, the doors locked while they were beaten up and robbed! A British bobbie (policeman) walking by heard their story and rushed down below, only to find the room empty. The perpetrators had exited out the back door never to be seen again. He shook his head saying that unfortunately these kinds of things happened far too often in this part of the city. Again, I received a late-night call from my husband, and again, we both knew Angels had been watching over him.

The third time was the most dramatic of all and occurred in the middle of the day rather than in the dark of night. My brother and I had terrible dreams about John dying in a plane crash just before he left on deployment after his third reenlistment. Both of us saw the same thing: John running from a burning plane like a human torch and crumbling to the tarmac. That is a traumatic dream to have just before your husband flies away, and for my brother to dream it too was doubly disturbing. By midmorning, I received a surprise in-air call from my husband. That had never happened before and appeared to be a special treat the crew was being given. We chatted lightly, and there was no warning inflection in his voice or manner. When I ended our conversation with "I'll see you when you get home," his answer was a little cryptic, and when I closed with a prayer for him, he added lightly, "Go ahead and pray for everyone else too!" ending with a strongly affirmative "I love you" before hanging up. The entire exchange lasted just minutes and gave me no clue that something was out of the ordinary aside from the surprise in-air call.

It wasn't until I'd hung up and walked across the room that it hit me.

He wasn't coming back. That was why they'd been allowed to call home. That was why he had encouraged me to pray for ALL of them! My legs felt weak under me, and I sat down to process what I was beginning to comprehend. The dream was happening! I'd had prophetic dreams before, but never one that directly affected me, and never one in tandem with my brother. Shaken to the core, I headed to the church to elicit others to pray with me; figuring that if GOD had let me know of the situation in advance, PRAYER could affect the final outcome. Otherwise, why tell me ahead of time? I'd seen the effects of midnight prayers for my husband in front of the Tabernacle in other circumstances and the remembrance of those times steadied my spirit.

By the time I reached the door of the sanctuary, I was in full battle mode! I enlisted the prayers of every soul I came across using the "two or more in His name" promise and hit my knees to engage in earnest. One of the souls that I fully expected to honor and engage in battle with me shocked me with their response, looking me in the eye and saying: "You don't *really* expect your prayers to *change* anything do you?!"

My response was immediate and visceral. My back straightened, my head lifted, and my eyes flashed as I declared, "I MOST CERTAINLY DO!"

I walked away from him and his disbelief and again went into battling mode, binding principalities, breaking strongholds, setting warrior Angels around the plane, asking divine wisdom for the pilots. After another hour of wrestling, an inner peace spread across my soul like a sweet balm easing heart and mind. It was settled. Whatever was going to happen was going to be IN HIS WILL, and I was good with that. I went home to wait.

Four hours later, the phone rang. My voice checked as I answered, and my spirit steadied for whatever voice would address me. My heart soared with relief at the sweet sound of my husband's voice telling me that they were safely on the ground. He thanked me softly, voice trembling slightly, for my prayers. The story was a harrowing one, in line with the dreams we'd had, and the plane landing safely was a true miracle. Yes. I believe GOD heard and answered the prayers. They MATTERED.

There had been a leak in the hydraulic system that rendered the landing gear and brakes inoperable. Everything on the aircraft that needed hydraulics to operate (flight controls, landing gear, and flaps) were compromised. The crew had to manually crank down the landing gear and flaps in order to get into proper configuration. There was no way to ensure the landing gear was fixed and locked, which heightened the risk of failure. They had circled for hours to empty the fuel tanks for the unavoidable emergency landing, choosing the longest runway to afford a path for coming in hot and fast.

As they were descending for the final approach the flight engineer had a brilliant idea of how to reroute some of the remaining hydraulic fluid into the landing gear and brake lines just before impact for a twenty-second assist with the landing. The tarmac had been foamed down for a possible crash-landing. Firetrucks were at the ready as the Boeing bird came in. The idea worked. They had just enough time to set the landing gear and just enough brakes to stop them before they hit the end of the runway! Pilots and crew literally ran from the plane in case the overheated brakes or tires exploded after such a hot landing.

It was a shaken and somber crew that disembarked that day, their dance with death still very much on every man's mind as they each called home to deliver the good news. That night, John and I held each other tight and thanked GOD for the privilege of doing so. As my husband fell into an exhausted sleep beside me, I continued my thanks and praise long into the night.

Chapter 17

The Calling

I had the sweet privilege of working with the youth. I started going to youth nights and subsequently formed a prayer group for the teens. We studied Scripture, prayed together, sang together, socialized together, grew spiritually in our shared love of the LORD; it was a very special time for all of us. Young people of course grow up and move, but the group itself faithfully gathered for fifteen years.

Another priest was assigned, and the youth ministry morphed as new rules emerged and new programs were embraced. In a surprise turn of events, I was approached to accept the position of paid youth minister. A position I had not applied for and was not interested in taking. I mentioned to our priest that I'd not applied for or even considered taking the position, and he quickly responded with "If it makes you feel any better, I never considered YOU for the position either!" He had chosen a young vibrant college student to serve, and when prompted to ask him who was the "holiest person" he knew, mine was the name that came up. And although this young man was hesitant to serve with me, our priest felt he was to ask me to consider doing so. I came back with "I need to pray about this" and told him I would let him know by the following Monday.

That Friday, we went to a friend's house in a neighboring state for a well-deserved weekend away, and it was there that GOD gave me an unequivocal answer to the question. During the initial tour of her home, I noted a very large St. Benedict's Medal hanging from a chain on her bedroom wall. I commented on how lovely it was, and she responded that a family friend (a deceased priest) had given it to her mother just before he died, and she had rescued it from a drawer in her mother's home. What she did not know is that I had a strong affection for St. Benedict (and his story of how he had withstood the attacks of the evil one from his own brothers in ministry) and knew well the Prayers of Protection that were engraved on both sides of the medal bearing his name. (Nor was she aware of the decision that I was in the process of making while in her home!)

She and her husband and John and I, had a lovely evening meal graced by one of the most perfectly executed Caesar salads anyone had ever made for us. We talked late into the night, sipping our wine and laughing often at the silliness of our own jokes, retiring only when it became beyond obvious we were all struggling to keep our eyes open!

The next morning, when I came down to breakfast, my friend had a funny look on her face. She greeted me with a soft whisper, "I almost woke you up at three in the morning!" Handing me a steaming hot cup of coffee, she began to tell me a story that instantly caught my attention.

Apparently at 3:00 a.m., the deceased priest appeared to her in a dream state, lifted the medal from the hook on the wall, handed it to her, and told her *she was to give it to ME*! With that revelation, *she laid the medal into my hand and said, "Take it. You are supposed to have it my friend!"* I was more than surprised. Aside from the strange and remarkable story, in one fell, swoop I had my answer. I was to say "yes" to the new position, and I would have the heavenly protection I needed to serve well. I put the medal on, and for as long as I served and wore it, there was no discord in the ministry.

Until the day, I took it off and it disappeared. Literally.

I was sitting on my couch at home as another tension headache threatened to overtake me, and I decided to remove the heavy necklace in an effort to stop the encroaching wave of pain. I "heard" a soft voice say, *"do not remove it or it will be lost"* and remember thinking "That's ridiculous, how can I lose it sitting on my COUCH?" I removed the weight from my tightened neck muscles and laid back. The pain receded, and I was able to carry on with my day. Interestingly enough, I never saw that medal again. *It was indeed lost.*

That very week all hell broke out in the ministry.

I needed to learn to heed those soft promptings whenever they came…to understand that they were not my own thoughts but rather heaven attempting to help me. Each time I had ignored them over the course of my life resulted in what could have been avoidable pain. Jesus's voice, God's voice, I knew—they were clear—ignoring their voice was impossible, but I was slowly learning that the angel voices were much softer and easier to pass off as my own "thoughts."

After six weeks of attempting on my own to navigate the dark, turbid waters that had been stirred up, I drove to a Benedictine monastery seeking to obtain another medal to replace the one I had lost. The medal I had been given had come through that very monastery, so in a way, I was coming full circle. As I entered the abbey, deep peace settled over me like a soft blanket, wrapping around and embracing my unsettled soul with a consolation I'd not felt before.

The medals they had for sale were all very small, and I bought two for my young grandchildren that had been complaining of night terrors. When I shared my story, the monk that was assisting me told me that there was an elderly priest that might be able to help and to wait there. Fifteen minutes later, he returned pushing a very old priest in a wheelchair. This one, too, listened to my story and with a soft voice and shaking hands offered to pray with me and give me His medal. Exactly like the one I'd lost in my refusal to listen to the angel's warning.

This one was on a brown leather cord instead of a chain, and as I put it over my head, I vowed to wear it whenever I was in youth minister mode. If it was not around my neck, it hung at the entryway to our home. My youth ministry days are long over, but that medal still hangs at the entryway of whatever house we are living in as a visual reminder to listen to my guardian angels and trust in heaven's provision. An interesting side-point, the night terrors ceased for both grandchildren as long as they wore the medals I had brought home that day.

In some ways, I was a rather poor choice for leading youth ministry. I had almost no computer or organizational skills, nor was I familiar with the necessity of creating yearly schedules far in advance or even more importantly, how to delegate. In the beginning, there was my assigned partner in ministry (the on-fire college student). Fortunately, my weaknesses were HIS strengths, and his weak areas became the places where I shined brightest. We were the perfect team, and the pastoral assistant to Father mentored us well. GOD richly blessed the years we served together. It was a wonderful time in both of our lives.

When he graduated and left to join the military, my weaknesses became evident as I struggled to keep up with the paperwork and ministry demands that were no longer being shared. I was overwhelmed by the workload and stressed. As more people came forward to serve, I admittedly did not know how to take full advantage of the gifts they brought with them. What I DID have was JESUS. In full measure. I knew how to reveal Him to others, how to invite Him into the room as we taught, and how to lead others into a meditative prayer. It was during these years that I had serious health hits that threatened to take me out. Every time I served a retreat or traveled with the teens I would suffer gravely upon our return. It almost seemed like the demonic realm was getting even for the spiritual advancements that were being made.

GOD called forth two wonderful ladies to love and serve with me in these difficult days, and a new team was born. These two women were written into the fabric of my being, becoming an integral part of the LIFE TEEN ministry and carrying the torch for many years, long after I retired and moved from the area. I look forward to dancing one day on heaven's shore with both of them!

Chapter 18

The Humbling

I served many years and became comfortable teaching the large groups of Lɪꜰᴇ Tᴇᴇɴ students that came every Sunday. The class was sixty-plus each week and the challenge of engaging so many and avoiding major distractions was one I enjoyed as it kept my lessons "fresh" and dynamically presented. In fact, after one particularly strong class I made the ʜᴜɢᴇ mistake of patting myself on the back and thinking, "I am a really ɢᴏᴏᴅ teacher" (Bɪɢ ᴍɪsᴛᴀᴋᴇ!)

The pushback was immediate and audible.

"Oh, ʀᴇᴀʟʟʏ?! Yᴏᴜ are!? Well then! Let's see just how ᴡᴇʟʟ you do ᴡɪᴛʜᴏᴜᴛ ᴍᴇ!"

It wasn't until the next Sunday's class that I began to understand the banner that had unfurled. Class was a *disaster.* I was well prepared; the lesson should have been engaging and interactive, but the teens were loud, distracted, and totally unengaged. The rest of the team spent their time trying to wrangle sixty-plus disinterested teens and keep a measure of control. It was not pretty.

The following Sunday was a repeat of the week before. I was beginning to understand that all my speaking and teaching "gifts" were seriously insufficient for such a large diverse group of youth, and my confidence in myself began to falter. The third Sunday's class put the nail in the coffin of my self-sufficiency. I found myself in the sanctuary on my knees afterward confessing my lack of understanding about Wʜᴏ actually was in control and ᴅᴏɪɴɢ the teaching.

It was not ME.

I had not realized the power of His presence in the classroom. I then humbly confessed the sin of pride and bowing low, invited THE TEACHER *back into our classroom.*

The following Saturday, I sat to research and prepare the lesson and was confounded. Nothing came forth, lesson plans that had flowed so easily for me before were slipping through my fingers, nothing catching or congealing, and I began to become desperate as the hour grew late. I heard the voice, this time gentle and kind, softly saying, *"I've GOT this."* I wasn't sure what that meant exactly, but I was exhausted by my ineffectual searching and decided to call it a night and go to BED. I got up early the next morning in an effort to gather and prepare something but again heard, even more clearly, *"I've got this."* As the time to depart grew nearer, I panicked and said aloud, "Okay, GOD, I hear You, but You have GOT to give me *SOMETHING!"* At which point my eyes were drawn to five separate items in the room with an interior prompting to collect and bring them with me. Once in the car, I was prompted to call ahead and ask them to set up a table in the front of the room and find a cloth to drape over the items I was bringing. I still had no idea what the class was going to be about, but at least, I wasn't walking in empty-handed. I arrived, the items were placed on the table and draped in white as our teens began to enter, and my mouth became dry as I realized I still had no idea of what would be taught that day.

My heart pounded as I greeted everyone and made the announcements, and in the space between the last announcement and the actual beginning of class, the download came. I literally received it all at once, understanding completely and began to teach authoritatively, uncovering and using the items I'd brought (one by one) to illustrate each particular point.

It was a powerful class. The funny part is that I don't remember the lesson. I was just the one speaking the words. The teens were riveted and fully focused on the lesson JESUS was teaching, and I felt honored to be the mouthpiece. I finally understood the process. The GLORY was all His! It was a HE-and-me dance, and I was loving learning to follow His lead!

The next Saturday while trying to prepare, I received the same message. This time, I responded more quickly and shut down my computer and headed to bed. In the morning, I inquired if I were to bring anything and was met with silence. On the way to the youth center, I "heard" instructions to set up our long tables in the shape of a cross and to drape pieces taken from our living stations of the cross box across it. Mary's blue veil, the disciple John's cloak, Jesus's crown of thorns, Simon's cloak, Pilate's robe and bowl, the hammer and nails. I was also instructed to have enough cord to give each teen a piece.

It was the beginning of LENT, and though I still had no "teaching," I felt comfortable with the direction we were headed. The teens entered quietly subdued by the unusual display that greeted them, and as I welcomed them in, the download began—the teaching was on life journeys and the questions asked, "Do you think those that walked with JESUS on the Way of Sorrows were *prepared* to do so? How does GOD prepare US for where we are being called to walk?" Each item again was woven effectively into the teaching, and it ended with each student being offered a cord and being invited to tie a knot for every unresolved issue in their lives especially those requiring *forgiveness*.

Lent was to be their time of preparation, and an opportunity to untie each knot was going to be given. I was shocked at how seriously they embraced the message, and the room was silent as they tied their knots. Years later, students came to me saying how profound an impact that exercise had made on them and on their experience of EASTER that year.

JESUS's lesson number 2 was a resounding success.

During my efforts to prepare the following week's lesson, I again heard a soft "*I got this*" and after a few more moments of looking online, closed out my computer, and went to bed sure that tomorrow's lesson was already taken care of. I got up the next morning refreshed and excited at the prospect of another surprise JESUS lesson and left for the youth center. I wanted to be there early enough to set up or prepare whatever was asked. *Only nothing was asked. No instructions were forthcoming.* As the clock ticked steadily toward our start time, nothing came to mind, and in the end, I stood before the class with the morning's announcements and welcoming greeting on my lips with no inclination of what was to come next!

Standing there in front of sixty-plus teenagers I screamed internally, "*What NOW, GOD?!*"

The response was immediate. "*Ask who here does martial arts.*"

I did. No response.

Internally, I cried out, "*Now what, GOD?*"

The response came quickly: "*Ask again!*"

I did. I countered that perhaps no one was doing it NOW, but there WAS someone in the room that had enrolled in martial arts classes at some point during their life! With great relief, I watched two teen boys raise their hands. I inquired what their disciplines were. One boy came back with "Jiu jitsu," and the other (a very shy quiet soul) answered, "Taekwondo." Now I know nothing about jiu jitsu, but my husband was a double black belt in taekwondo, and I had been to a few competitions and classes with him; this discipline I knew! I asked my shy young man to come forward as I internally inquired of the Teacher:

"*What now?*"

"*Tell him to do his form.*"

I faced him, bowed with a sharp "Cha-ryut" greeting (which means "Attention"), and he responded in kind. I then instructed him to do his form. My shy boy responded with a rapid and emphatic "I can't..." as a true deer in the headlights look came across his face.

Inside I'm beginning to panic and I say, "*WHAT NOW, LORD?*" as I sense the kid's growing discomfort.

I was quite surprised to hear with increased intensity: "*Ask again!*"

I turned and uttered a sharper "Cha-ryut" and, again, with greater intensity asked him to do his form. The panic on his face was evident as he looked side to side for relief and again cried out in dismay, "I CAN'T! IT'S BEEN TOO LONG! I DO NOT REMEMBER IT...I DON'T REMEMBER IT!"

Now I am the one in dismay!

I am the one panicking as I cry out in my spirit:

"*What am I supposed to do now, Lord!?*"

"*Command Him to do His form!*" resounded loudly in my head!

I turned to face my poor boy once again, *this time COMMANDING in the LOUD AUTHORITATIVE VOICE of a MASTER*—"Do. Your. Form."

Quite suddenly, he collected himself, pulled into starting stance and delivered the entire form PERFECTLY to a room collectively holding its breath as he glided through the movements.

He finished to a roar of applause that changed his status in the class forever, as JESUS dropped the rest of the teaching into my astonished mind.

The bottom line was the question, "Why was he finally able to do his form when he was hard pressed?" The jiu jitsu student's hand quickly shot up as he emphatically stated, "Because *he* PRACTICED IT over and over and OVER!" It was written in him.

The final point downloaded that very moment. THAT IS WHY we "practice" our faith. Learning daily how to live it out and live it out better and better so that when we are pushed up against adversity it will not fail us—we draw deep on what is written *in* us! The recognition of this great truth flashed across the faces sitting in the room in front of me, and I silently gave GOD kudos for an absolutely STUNNING lesson!

The next week, when I sat down to prepare, ideas and thoughts again flowed, and grace guided the lesson plan. Never again would I assume that I was in charge of the lesson or the delivery. Never again would I take credit for how a lesson impacted the hearts that were called that day to hear. This new understanding washed over every area of my life, and in a sense, I was once again a new creation. I began to let go of the reins, allowing others to step forward and teach, knowing that HE could do whatever He wanted in and through their efforts. I no longer needed to be in control. HE was the Great Teacher, not me, and He was writing in their lives as well as mine!

It was after this great lesson that GOD became silent for a very long while. For nearly two years, I moved only in the faith that He was still there without feeling His presence or hearing His voice. It was a time of great sorrow for me as I had grown dependent on

His constant presence in my days! I longed to feel His solace, and as the months flowed into years, I just continued to serve, teach, go to Mass, and sing…without consolation. Near the end of this period (what the saints refer to as the "dark night of the soul") I found myself questioning everything—all my beliefs, everything that I had experienced, indeed, the very existence of the God I taught and proclaimed!

It was then I remembered the Cabbie's words proclaimed over me and my friend forty years previously when he told us we would not always bask in God's presence, "GOD IS STILL THERE. *Regardless of what you feel. Hold onto that.*"

I HELD ON. The dark night ended, and GOD started showing up again, picking up where we had left off with a new, even sweeter intimacy than I remembered. I was grateful that I had not listened to the dark voices that told me, "God is not real," "There is no reason to stay," "Why are you still here?" "Nothing you do matters. YOU don't matter!" nor given in to the discouragement that marked my days for those two years of suffering.

Chapter 19

Queen of Hearts

Three steps forward, two steps back. That seemed to be my spiritual cadence. The good news was that I kept moving forward like a child following a path laid out with small treasures carefully hidden from view but each one more easily discovered. The understanding was if I would seek, I would find. He would never again "hide" from me, and it became a delightful game between us. I loved being available whenever He called, and He would often connect me with another soul needing direction or comfort. As I got better at hearing, the sendings came more often. Crossroads Mall became a place I was called to so often that I began to call it Mall Church—cheerily calling out to my husband whenever beckoned into service: "Off to Mall Church! Catch you later!" We started calling the impromptu meetings "divine appointments."

One Sunday afternoon in response to a prompting, I found myself walking through the downstairs portion of the mall looking at storefronts and the people passing, trying to discern who the next divine appointment was. My eyes were drawn to a young, rather harried-looking woman with a baby carriage waiting outside a men's clothing store. "*Her.*" No other message. Just "her." I walked over to the carriage and began to engage the little one—a cherubic, curly-dark-haired baby girl with flashing eyes. She looked over my right shoulder and laughed, then over my left, and laughed again!

Her mother immediately turned in shock and said to me, "I cannot believe she is laughing with you! She absolutely hates strangers and always cries if someone she doesn't know approaches her! WHO are you?!" At which point, I laughed at the absurdity of it all and exclaimed that her little one was not playing with ME but with my guardian angels, and the "GOD-window" opened.

We had a short conversation about her recent desire expressed in bedtime prayer to "get right with GOD" and go back to Church. GOD then expressed HIS desire to have her do just that and gently invited her to make it sooner rather than later! At that point, her husband returned (also surprised by his little one's continued joy in my presence), and she quickly brought him up to speed. They walked away hand in hand, tears in their eyes, daughter still happily chortling in her carriage as they agreed GOD had sent them an unmistakable message! I headed back toward my car and felt myself being detoured through the perfume section of Dillard's to engage a young woman there.

Conversation between us started easily but quickly went deep. She was mourning the loss of her mother earlier that year (today was her mother's birthday), and she found herself longing for a sign of some kind to give her hurting spirit solace. I stopped and prayed with her right there in the store, and a sweet peace settled over us both! A big smile came from deep inside, opening her face like a flower to sunlight making my heart dance. I loved Mall Church!

GOD continued to leave me sweet treasures along these secret paths of His, and I opened up more and more of my time for the divine appointments that consistently appeared. It was at a business conference in Phoenix that the ultimate trifecta occurred that would lock in the idea of setting aside time for divine appointments.

The morning had begun with worship at the request of conference attendees (it was Sunday), and the prayer and worship had been intense. It was a nondenominational gathering, and all were encouraged to come. After the service, several groups of two began praying over those who asked. I stood in a line, and a young man raised his hands over my head and began to pray. All of a sudden, he stopped, looked at me, and told me that he didn't know how to interpret what he was seeing. He saw a large chess piece over me very clearly. The *queen*. As he searched for significance, he offered that perhaps it meant that I could move with power in any direction. I walked away and as I did, another lady approached asking if I needed prayer. I shook my head, assuring her that I had already been prayed over but stopped short when she looked at me intently, uttering with soft amusement, "Oh *no*...you are not done yet...there is MORE. GOD has more. Let me finish the prayer!"

Obediently, I stepped forward, bowed my head and she began her prayer. She, too, saw the queen chess piece, followed by a chrysalis splitting open and a butterfly crawling out, wings not yet unfurled. She proclaimed that my ministry as His little queen was beginning, and that very quickly, my wings would open, and I would learn to FLY! A large smile crossed over her face as she hugged me and wished me well, releasing me back into the world to find my place.

I hurried back to the huge conference room, aware that I was late, searching for my group and unable to locate anyone. Walking up one more aisle in search of them, a man called out to me, "Are you looking for a seat? There is one right here!" motioning to the open space beside him.

I slid in beside him as the morning program began, and we introduced ourselves. During the break, he told me his rather interesting (and unusual) story. He had come down to the conference from Canada and had been detained at the border in a case of mistaken identity as a *murder suspect* accused of murdering his wife! It took several hours to settle that he was NOT *that person* and be released, only to be stopped again by a highway patrol stateside with the same accusation and another roundabout-figure-out before he was released again. Then crossing the Arizona border, he had a flat tire—a complete blowout requiring a tow—and had nearly turned around and gone back home. All of a sudden, clear as day, I received a message from heaven for him and requested permission to give it. He answered, "Of course!" and I began to speak: "*You were chosen for ministry many years ago and refused your calling. It is waiting for you.*"

A distinct pause...followed by *"It is time."*

I then offered that Satan had done everything in his power to keep him from getting here to receive this message. Tears flooded his eyes as his face flushed red, and he acquiesced that my message was accurate; he had indeed been called by God into ministry many years ago and had refused choosing a secular life instead. More then came:

"You are out of time. You are to turn now, go back and say 'YES' to God's call on your life."

He grabbed my shoulders, looked me in the eye—soul to soul—and thanked me, promising to DO just that, picking up his belongings and leaving. He had gotten what he had come for!

The unfurling of wings had begun!

I found my group at the end of the day, only to find that they were headed to HOOTERS; after the way my day was unfolding, HOOTERS seemed like a poor choice, so I went on alone.

Walking through the hotel, I noted two gentlemen marked with name tags as being conference members and engaged them in conversation, asking if they knew of a good place to eat close by. They did and offered a place at their table if I wanted to join them!

We had a delightful dinner and were enjoying our conversation when one of the men's phone alarms went off, signaling an appointment. They had planned to go to a small group meeting together back at the conference center. When pressed, the gentleman to my right declined, saying that he wanted to finish our conversation and would catch up to him later.

We continued to talk about ourselves, the world, the ins and outs of life, and how people miss opportunities. He gave me some personal background as we chatted (he was a lawyer) and recounted an experience of being misjudged during his final year at Yale. He was presenting an oral thesis on whether or not Affirmative Action had been a positive move forward—as he was delineating his position—the professor stopped him with great disdain and disgust, declaring, "EASY for YOU to say, born with a SILVER SPOON in your mouth and everything given on a silver platter!" shutting down his speech and the point he was making.

Regrouping, he shot back with the fact that indeed there had been NO silver spoon *or* platter. His parents had been drug addicts, and he had spent the first seven years of his life locked in a closet, routinely beaten and covered with cigarette burns given in games of "Don't you dare cry."

Pulled out by DHS after a neighbor's report, his life turned another corner. He was raised in successive foster homes and released back into society at the age of eighteen. He had made his own way through school, working part-time jobs, earning merit scholarships, finally being accepted at Yale. The professor dropped his attack, silenced by the truth, and he finished his oral dissertation to a room so quiet you could have heard a pin drop.

One of my gifts is spiritual discernment. I can usually spot someone who has been traumatized, but I had not noted anything around this man. He seemed "clean." I offered that he must have found some way to forgive his parents as he didn't seem to be carrying any darkness with him.

"I did what I needed to do to move on" was his response.

All of a sudden, heaven was speaking, and I had an outrageous message for him. Had I not been sure of what I was hearing, I would never have dared to deliver it.

Gingerly, I inquired, "Are you a God person?"

He looked up and said, "If you are asking if I believe in God, I do, but I don't do religion."

I locked eyes with him and declared that I had a message I believed was from God and requested his permission to deliver it.

Keeping his eyes locked on mine, he responded carefully, "Okay."

I opened my mouth to deliver the message but the incongruity of it almost stopped the words from coming out; only the faith I had in what I was hearing and WHO was giving it kept me going.

"Your parents didn't DO it."

Now the thoughts were raging inside me: *Of COURSE they had! They had locked him up, abused him, and abandoned him.* How could those be words from heaven?!

Then the rest of the message downloaded: *"The demonic bondage of drugs and abuse was passed down generation to generation, the spiritual bondage becoming greater and greater with each passing generation.*"

He shook his head yes, saying it went back all the way to his great grandfather. Now I was sure of the message I was receiving and gave the final piece with complete confidence.

"*You need to understand, it was far too strong, impossible for your parents to stand against. THEY did not do it. It was the demonic realm that took such delight in torturing you as a child.*"

We both got goosebumps and he began to cry softly as the final piece settled in, healing his little-boy broken heart. Now full forgiveness was possible. Complete. He could move on.

We sat together silently for several minutes and then got up to head back to the hotel.

Walking out the front door we were immediately confronted by a homeless drug addict looking for a handout. His response, born out of habit, was to wave him aside, but then looking my direction, he reconsidered and gave him a few dollars. The scruffy young man then turned to me, avoiding my gaze but asking if I could spare anything. He was unkempt, smelly, and as I got closer, I thought I perceived what might be lice in his long greasy hair. I opened my purse, told him I needed $15 to travel with tomorrow, but anything else was his. As I collected the money and reached over to press it into his outstretched hand, I heard, "*Tell him it is from ME and that I love him.*"

As I leaned toward him, I said, "This might sound weird—but this is from JESUS and He wants you to know He Loves you." The young man looked up and over my shoulder, expressionless, still avoiding looking me in the eye (something I now know is connected to demonic oppression), taking the proffered bills and shoving them into a pocket.

"*HUG HIM.*"

WHAT!? Hug him?! He was dirty. He smelled. HE MIGHT HAVE LICE!

But when JESUS tells you to hug someone, you do it. I held my breath and leaned in to hug him. A real HUG. A long HUG. A JESUS HUG.

When I finally let go and pulled back, his eyes were clear, and he locked eyes with mine, smiling for the first time during our encounter. He shared his convoluted story, how he ended up on the streets, and how he was afraid to go home. JESUS again spoke telling him that it was time to go home. All would be forgiven. He had a promise and a FUTURE that he needed to bravely walk into. His shoulders straightened, his head lifted—all of a sudden he no longer looked downtrodden or quite so scruffy. A genuine smile flashed across his face and his eyes glistened like morning stars!

My lawyer friend looked astonished but said nothing as we walked away. I realized we were not done yet. We needed backup in the spirit realm, and I searched the surrounding area for someone that might be able to assist. In front of the hotel was a tall, dark, very noble-looking uniformed guard standing watch, and I heard internally *"Him."*

By this point, I was beyond questioning anything, so I marched right up to him and inquired, "Are you a GOD man?"

He nodded yes and looked at me questioningly, as I blurted out all that had happened in our previous encounter. He immediately went into policeman mode heading the direction I had indicated when I stopped him: "NO. That is not what is needed. I need someone to PRAY with me! I need coverage for his soul while he makes his way back home to break any strongholds that might try to stop him! Can you PRAY with me?"

His face changed. Softened. His answer was wrapped in a heavy accent.

"I can pray. But not in English. It is not my language. I am from Nigeria."

His uniformed shoulders squared, and his back straightened.

"I will pray in my tongue."

We joined hands and began as my new lawyer friend watched incredulously. The prayers flowed out from our centers, weaving around us, making where we stood sacred space. All of a sudden, my Nigerian policeman was praying in ENGLISH; his eyes opened wide (as did mine), and we both became aware that something very special was happening! He was *speaking* in Nigerian, and yet we were both *hearing* it in English! We knew then our PRAYERS had reached heaven and would be answered. The battle was over. We hugged joyously, no longer officer and civilian, but a warriors-in-the-spirit duo. We smiled and parted, he going back to his post, me going up to my room, and my lawyer friend presumably to *his* room to have a long talk with God about everything! And yes, once I got to my room, I immediately showered and washed my hair, scrubbing my head *twice*, praying that I would be "lice less" in the morning!

(As I am sure you have already guessed. I was.)

As I lay in the dark looking up at a ceiling I could not see, I asked GOD why He was talking to me in these ways. He answered that I was His little queen of golden arrows—that with my help, He could shoot arrows of truth and healing into the hearts of souls, and the tears they cried were signs that the arrows had hit their mark!

I liked being called His little queen.

I liked shooting his golden arrows.

It was in that moment the seeing of the queen chess piece made sense. And the chrysalis opening. The butterfly wings unfurling. All of it made sense.

I could hardly wait for tomorrow.

I slept.

Chapter 20

The Adventure Continues

The next day, I was to fly back home, but my husband had booked my flight for late in the afternoon to allow time for more divine appointments. During the conference, I had come across a group of men in the lunchroom speaking with easily identified accents. Irish. I'm of Irish heritage, and after living in Ireland for a time in my youth, I could muster a fine Irish brogue myself.

I entered into the conversation, and they commented that it was a MUST that I visit the Irish Cultural Center in town before I left to go back home. I had awakened early, and having plenty of time for an outing, decided to take their advice and make a detour on my way to the airport. The Shuttle driver agreed to drop me off in front of the center with my luggage—and it wasn't until he had driven away that I noticed the CLOSED MONDAY sign. It was already over one hundred degrees, and I was pretty much in the middle of a concrete jungle.

Now what? The butterfly within was unconcerned with the change in plan—willing to spread her wings and turn into the wind. Even with luggage in hand! It was a new feeling, and I embraced the freedom to just *be* in the moment without an agenda of my own. I looked under the low bridge in front of me and saw a group of workers…them? No. Nothing. I looked the opposite direction across a large field connected to the cultural center's property and saw a lone figure moving quickly across the expanse. Him? Affirmative. *"Him."*

I turned and began walking, angling my path to coincide with his trajectory. We met in the middle, and he greeted me with a deep Irish brogue, I responded with a cheeky "Top o' the mornin' to ya!" He chuckled and stopped to chat. I told him my dilemma, and he laughed again!

"Ya have NO idea of who I am do ya?!" I shook my head and he proceeded to inform me that he was the caretaker of the cultural center and was on his way over for his daily walk-through!

A personal tour was offered and accepted—and there I was—on my way into the Irish Cultural Center after all! It seemed I walked with a GOD that could open any door.

The tour was engaging, my tour guide charming as we moved through the center, from room to room, and he regaled me with Gaelic tales and stories of the Irish in this city. The tour ended as we arrived in the gift shop, but our conversation continued. As I fingered the beautiful ornate rosaries, he mentioned that he had been Catholic once, but had not been in a church for many years, and the window opened for the butterfly to fly through. I told my story of coming back via the mission priest that had been pulled off the street to be Christ to me, and some of the miracles that followed, including my healing and restoration to my husband. Some part of the story touched him deeply, resounding in his spirit as JESUS breathed His love-call over him, and despite the fact there was no direct message, a message had indeed been received. Tears filled his eyes as he declared that I had given him a great gift and that he wanted to give ME one in return! "Anything in the store is yours—just choose it! I will buy it for you!" I picked the green ornate rosary that I had fingered earlier, and he lit up with excitement—"DONE!"

Going back out onto the street, I was hit with a shimmering wave of heat as my shoes threatened to stick to the hot pavement below. He provided directions to a nearby restaurant as I still had time before I needed to head for the airport. I snaked my way down and across each block trying to catch every scrap of shade I could find along the way! Once there, I went into the air-conditioned coolness and ordered a salad. On my way out, I was stopped by an apparent altercation in the lobby between a finely dressed, officious, heavyset woman, and the sweet, young, slightly flustered hostess: "You need to *do* something about the panhandler outside your establishment! Call the police and get him taken away! Now!" As the little hostess reluctantly turned toward the phone on the wall; the woman raised herself up, huffed loudly, and walked out the door allowing it to slam emphatically behind her. I leaned across, lightly touching the hostess's shoulder as her hand picked up the receiver and offered, "How about I just buy him a meal instead?" Her eyes widened gratefully, and she nodded with a soft smile of acquiescence: "That would be wonderful!"

Outside, our panhandler was one door-stoop over—obviously hot, thin, and hungry-looking. He just wanted a bowl of spaghetti and a glass of water. Nothing more. I walked back into the air-conditioning, placed his order, paid for it, and got permission for him to come in and eat. As I was walking back out to bring him in, a lady moved from a hidden spot behind a potted plant catching my eye, saying, "I saw everything. All of it. Start to finish. Thank you."

She then disappeared as quickly as she had appeared. It was as if GOD had seen and wanted me to know.

Bringing our man in to sit in the cool to eat his meal, I offered a "blessing" and hope for the morrow. He responded, eyes downcast, with a humble "Thank you for your kindness. I can never repay you." My response was immediate: "You do not have to repay me, one day, YOU will pay this kindness forward just as I have." *A bowl of spaghetti now paid for by a grilled cheese sandwich provided for me so many years ago when I had been homeless and hungry.* His eyes filled with tears as his food arrived, and I left, feeling that his life was indeed changed *like mine had been,* even though—like my young homeless man of yesterday—I would not have the privilege of watching his story play out.

Looking at my watch, I realized it was time to go. As I stepped back into the heat, a cab appeared and allowed me to hail it. What were the odds? Living in the kingdom, the odds were in my favor. Yes. Very much in my favor.

When a priest asked me years later what my calling was, I declared, "To be *available.*" He stiffened, sniffed and said, *"That's* not a calling!" To which I replied (with a short laugh) that indeed it was…and very few were willing to step into the position.

My days were planned and now written in pencil. GOD held the eraser and I gave Him complete freedom to erase and rewrite His little queen's days as HE saw fit. He used my willingness to yield often—changing the course of many of my days and turning my life into a wonderful adventure of "Turn heres," "Stop theres," "Sit in that chair," and "Talk to that one over there!" In retrospect, it very much feels like how a butterfly must feel as it flies, lifted by wind currents, changing direction easily and enjoying each fragrant encounter highlighted with sweet sips of nectar! This was a way of living that I found easy to do and hard to explain.

Bars, restaurants, parks, shopping malls, bathrooms, conference centers; all became places of divine appointments, each new day a doorway to a new GOD-adventure. I quickly became aware of just HOW connected our GOD is to his people, even when they are unable to see or hear him. That said, there were times the appointment was not so much for *them* as it was for *me*.

Two immediately come to mind. The first was after a short testimony talk I had been invited to give to a church group. A woman walked up, face alight, saying that she had been inspired by my story—at the same time lamenting that GOD had not revealed Himself so clearly or granted any big miracles in *her* life—sighing, "You must be very SPECIAL to the LORD!"

Okay. I admit it. In that moment, I thought to myself, *I suppose I am special.*

The reprimand from heaven was immediate and admonished my spirit soundly: *"OH, you ARE special all right! So very special*—with the rest of His intention suddenly downloading into my chastened spirit! Gently, He reminded me, *"Many of My children do not see what you have seen, yet they still BELIEVE and proclaim My goodness. If you had not SEEN and HEARD, you might have been LOST! I give each of my children exactly what they need to FIND and KNOW Me."* He showed me how much PLEASURE *He takes* in those faithful souls that follow without great signs or wonders to lead them, *how pleasing they are to Him,* and I felt my soul humbling within me.

I was no longer proud of being "special." In fact, I was now deeply aware of how truly special, how infinitely precious those who do NOT see and yet believe and TRUST in Him are. It truly flipped how I saw everyone else in an instant. The last shall be first. OUCH. Now whenever I share parts of my story, I make sure to let everyone know how our GOD sees and loves them as they are!

The second time was at a LIFE TEEN youth conference. I had gone with another youth minister to learn about the program, and we were attending our first LIFE TEEN Mass. The air was thick with JESUS, and it felt like the worship music wrapped us up and delivered us to the foot of the THRONE. We were both on our knees, side by side, praying—deep in communion with our God—when I heard Him say softly with great admiration over her: *"Isn't she beautiful?"* Then even more tenderly, *"She's my FAVORITE."*

My shock was palpable. My head lifted in surprise.

I thought *I* was His FAVORITE. Worse, the person kneeling beside me was a challenge for me to understand or like; we were so very different! Like oil and water, we did not mix, so for HER to be His FAVORITE was a reflection of Him that I did not get. As I knelt, now thoroughly confused and humbled, JESUS kindly revealed the rest to my aching soul—*we are ALL His FAVORITES—He loves EACH, fully and completely in the moment as if THEY ARE THE ONLY ONES.* He fully knows and sees our "ugly" and declares us HIS and BEAUTIFUL.

As I wrapped my mind around the incredible beauty of those truths and the import of it on all of humanity, I recognized that my understanding of WHO GOD WAS had been very small and so painfully limiting. I still had *so* much to learn! Learning to really "see" and love that soul that had knelt beside me that day *was one of them*, and I did. We had some deep heart-to-heart conversations while we were there as I looked deeper into "who' this person was that GOD loved so dearly that He would make a point of telling me!

She was my first teacher of the grace of seeing another with God-eyes. While our differences kept us from being close buddies, she definitely continued to be my sister-in-Christ, and we were always delighted to see one another whenever our paths crossed. She is dear to me even to this day!

Chapter 21

The Coming

John and I spent twenty-two years cocooned in grace while the evil one continued to attack, stirring up issues with family, health, and finances. GOD always provided illumination and a way out. In one notable instance, I was provided the information I needed to survive *before* the attack. I had picked up a *Redbook* magazine on a whim, an article about a new mother of twins that lost one arm and both legs to a "flesh-eating virus" catching my attention. I had medical training while in the navy, and these types of stories fascinated me.

She told her story in great detail, outlining the timeline and how all the pieces had fallen together. The medical system had failed her, missing the cues, sending her home. By the time her husband got her back to the hospital the next morning, it was too late. They saved her life, but not her limbs. For a mother of newborn twins, it was horrific.

Two days later, her story became a part of mine.

I had just finished cooking dinner and setting it on the table when a wave of nausea, weakness, and pain in my left arm made me retreat to my room. I took off my top and noted a purply blue patch about the size of an orange on my inner upper arm. It ached, unlike anything I had ever experienced before, and I had a horrible feeling that something was terribly wrong. I told my husband that he needed to take me to hospital. I was SICK. He protested that we had not even eaten yet, but one look at my stricken face convinced him to forget the food and get me there.

As we drove, I remembered the article I had read and the time-line she had shared. She, too, had been hit at dinnertime. She, too, had an unusual purply blue rash on her left arm that ached. She, too, had felt desperately ill without explanation. When I got to the hospital, they took my vitals and the ER physician diagnosed acute cellulitis, wrote a prescription and attempted to send me home. That was exactly what had happened to my *Redbook* mom, and she'd nearly not survived.

I was determined not to make the same mistake.

I told the doctor, "I am sicker than you think I am, and I am not going anywhere!" He replied that insurance would not pay for me to stay, and again, I refused to leave, saying I would lie in the parking lot if I had to, but I was not going home. The doctor relented, saying I could stay for thirty more minutes, and then I would be sent home. During the next thirty minutes, my temperature rose to 104, my arm doubled in size, my blood pressure bottomed out, my pulse skyrocketed, and my white blood cell count went over fifty thousand. The doctor's face became serious as he echoed my earlier words: "You are right, you are not going anywhere!" He started calling out directions to the attending nurses.

Antibiotics were started via IV. I was admitted immediately and checked every ten minutes for infection progression. I believe God inspired the doctor's choice of antibiotics and miraculously stopped the infection cold in its tracks. My refusal to leave, and his quick response when things went south, kept what could have been deadly lassoed in. A goat rodeo without casualties.

I spent four days in the hospital. Lots of doctors and nurses came through to "view my case" as I was an anomaly, both in what HAD happened and in what had NOT. I lost no tissue, which in and of itself was remarkable as these infections move quickly and are usually hard to stop. Once I returned home, I took the time to locate and write the *Redbook* article author and thanked her for saving my life. She called me and we cried together—sisters bound by a shared experience, though her journey had been and continues to be, far more difficult.

That hospitalization was the first of many hits. John's son came to live with us and immediately went to the dark side. Hanging with wannabe gangbangers, adopting the uniform of cap and baggy-saggy pants, staying out late and constant encounters with the police were no surprise. It was a tight fit in the house with five of us in a small four bedroom, and ill-spirits found it easy to stir the pot, raising stress levels for everyone. My brother became angrier, reclusive, and nonverbal.

My daughter began to seek a way out "to live on her own" and was working a job and going to college at the same time. As she jumped into her new life on her own, rabbit holes opened everywhere and like *Alice in Wonderland*, she fell in. That was the end of our idyllic mother-daughter relationship and the beginning of a stressful not so successful maneuvering through all the baggage we both carried from the divorce that we had so nimbly avoided until now. She moved out, and John's son returned to his mother. Then there were three.

John made chief and had the opportunity to stay and try for senior chief or retire and begin with a new start-up company that recruited him personally. He chose to retire. A new life was beginning. My brother continued to be difficult, so we decided to build a house. A bigger house, giving him his own area with a small bedroom, office, bathroom, private porch, and garage workshop for his woodworking and us some privacy. He hated it. It was the beginning point for a long downward spiral. We were fighting a battle we could not win. What we did not know at the time is that we weren't *meant* to. Like my first husband was for me, we were merely a protective holding ground for my brother. He eventually would win his own war.

Summer of cats - the first set of growing spring babies.

GOD gently closes the door with the flowers from CHEWY.

The prophetic pastel painting.

Madonna and child painted upon my return from Medjugorje. This painting hung in a Church for 13 years, and now rests in the home of a dear friend.

So many grave tragedies struck our nation in a relatively short space of time. The next ten-year period brought five biggies: First came the World Trade Center bombing in New York City on February 26, 1993, killing six people. It was our first real terrorist attack on American soil. I remember being shaken by it. Feeling vulnerable. I remember praying with the teens and feeling that more was coming and that we needed to be prepared spiritually for what was to come. The global alarm clock was ringing. We as a people hit the proverbial snooze button. Life went on.

I'd begun painting again, and late one night two years later, felt compelled to get up and paint a life-sized self-portrait. Dressed in nightgown and bathrobe, rosary in hand, looking up to heaven with tears streaming down my face, the image was one of sorrow and anguish. Rendering it in soft pastels, I completed it in two days. Three days later on April 19, 1995, I woke up. Walking outside, I saw my neighbors in the street, talking—the shock on their faces drawing me over still in my bathrobe to hear the news. The Murrah Building in downtown OKC had just been bombed. Later, I learned 163 people instantly died (including nineteen children in the day care center), eighty-three were hospitalized, and 319 were injured. And yes, I prayed my rosary, eyes raised to heaven, tears streaming down my face. My painting all of a sudden took on a much different meaning. It had been prophetic.

On May 3, 1999, another mega tragedy occurred. The state of Oklahoma was crushed under a huge tornadic mega-event spawning twenty EF-4 and EF-5 tornadoes. Almost six hundred went to ER or were hospitalized, thirty-six people died, over 2,500 homes were destroyed or severely damaged. So many were mentally and financially devastated by this overwhelming storm that literally scoured the ground clean leaving only cement foundations where houses once stood. So many stories of miraculous survival and a wondrous response from the rest of the country brought solace and HOPE.

On September 11, 2001, a series of four coordinated suicide terrorist attacks took down New York City's Twin Towers killing 2,996 people. Many of us watched the horror unfold in real time as the second plane hit, people jumping from windows and the final crumbling of the tower, blanketing New York City and its people in ash. What was our world coming to? As we waited for reports of survivors found under the wreckage, many began praying. Churches filled, and as long as the process was in motion, people prayed hard. Unfortunately, once the last living soul was declared found, New York City (and our country) slowly went back to business and the churches emptied out once again. We were being warned, but no one was paying attention.

On May 8, 2003, another EF-4 Tornado tore through the Oklahoma town of Moore, officially making Moore "Tornado Alley." Then on December 26, 2004, the biggest event of all hit—a 9.2 submarine earthquake hit off the coast of Indonesia triggering a deadly tsunami in the Indian Ocean that hit thirteen countries, killing over 226,000 people in a hit so hard the entire planet vibrated, triggering aftershocks as far away as Alaska. People watched livestream videos in horror as entire communities were swept away in an instant. We literally watched thousands die on TV, and it was not a movie. It was REAL.

The next Sunday found me in church on my knees before Mass praying and asking JESUS if this was "it"—if HE was coming, if what I had seen in Thailand had been the Thessalonian reference of two in a field—one taken, one left behind. I had watched the news in horror as some were swept away by the rushing waters, others left behind. His reply was soft and measured: *"I am coming."*

Not strong or end-of-times powerful. No lion of Judah roar. Just a soft, measured, *"I am coming."* To be quite honest, I didn't know what to *do* with that response, so I just let it go. Mass started, and I entered the prayer not understanding whether or not my question had even been answered. I continued my routine of prayer group, rosary group, and daily Masses with a sense that something more was coming; I just had no idea WHAT.

The following Sunday found me in the front pew early (as an assigned Eucharistic minister) deep in prayer. As I entered into conversation with GOD, head bowed, the entire church (including the pew in front of me) disappeared. GONE. I was in a new space. This was different from anything I had ever seen or experienced before.

My downcast eyes were gazing at the most BEAUTIFUL FEET *I had ever seen. I saw the nail holes and immediately knew whose feet I was seeing…* WHO *was standing in front of me…* JESUS.

My gaze lifted, I noted the rough weave of his linen garment and the simple cord tie at his waist, *but those* FEET, *those beautiful, beautiful feet.* They drew my gaze back down and in adoration I laid my face on them, truly understanding for the first time why someone would weep over them, pour perfume on them, and then dry them with their hair; *of course she would,* of course *I would!* I wanted to stay there, my head on those beautiful feet, forever.

The bell announcing the start of Mass startled me, and the church began to reclaim the space around me and pews and people reappeared. I cried out to JESUS: "Don't GO—let me stay with my head on your feet somehow, *at least for the duration of the Mass!*" I don't know how…but somehow, I felt that I stayed there with him in that space even while I stood, sat, kneeled, and served the mass. HE HAD COME as He had said.

I HAD TOUCHED HIM.

What do you *do* with an event like that? Who do you tell? A skeptical priest? A close friend? Initially, I told no one except my husband. The next week brought another visit, this time not a change in *space*, but rather in *substance*. I came to church early hoping for another encounter, but the Mass was normal up until communion. As I came forward in line, I felt a stirring deep inside of me, an "awareness," but of what? When my turn came, the "what" was unmistakable! The uplifted host in front of me was shining with *GLORY LIGHT*; *it was JESUS*, revealing Himself in a remarkable way.

I was so overcome that I just *stood* there staring in awe. There was a long, sweet moment before the priest extended his arm and placed JESUS on my tongue. As I walked back to my pew, the bread became like flesh, and I tasted a sweetness that was hard to put in words. I had known that He was truly present in Eucharist, but this was the first time that I was allowed to *taste* His divine presence. *Indeed, HE had COME.*

TWICE.

These divine encounters gave me great encouragement and strength in what proved to be very difficult times: estrangement from my daughter, my brother's crash and burn, and within the year, my being set free for a new ministry. It was during this time that we had begun attending midweek charismatic prayer meetings at a small local nondenominational church. We found comfort in the strength of the worship and prayer time there and went often.

The worship style was very different from the structured formal ritualized Mass, and at first it was a little disconcerting. As we met the people there and heard their stories of healing and deliverance, we became intrigued, and the raised hands and shouts of "Praise the LORD!" midservice no longer seemed so incongruous with serious worship. It was here that I watched people raise their hands and call down the power of GOD and souls walk away changed. It was here that I learned to stand up in the spirit in a new way.

It was in September of 2009 that I became aware that the world was unraveling somehow, and time was unraveling with it. I found myself running from place to place, job to job, duty to duty going just fast enough to "make it," but never feeling ahead of the game or secure. There was *so* much chaos and unhappiness—so much sickness and death all around me. The attacks of the evil one on God's children were becoming bolder, and the calls for intercessory prayer came daily. Little did we know that MUCH worse was yet to come!

September 10 was a difficult day full of very real challenges and spiritual attacks from all sides! I began to pray deeply for all the souls I knew were struggling. When I interceded for the pastor of the little local church and his wife, I felt a shift in the spiritual realm and I knew internally that the rest of the day would end up being interesting. And indeed, it was. Conflict at the senior center during my art class, a crisis with our newest CORE team members in the youth ministry, my coministers both under attack, my brother and husband butting heads. WHAT A DEVILISH DAY!

As I stood the gap interceding for the pastor's wife and her husband, I felt a "push" back from the spiritual realm, almost a challenge, an "*Oh yeah? You want to stand HERE?!*"

It was intimidating, and I almost "sat down" and turned away. Inexplicably, I felt a surge of confidence realizing that I had been training for this moment for my whole life, internally declaring, I would NOT sit down or back away. I would STAND in CHRIST, stand the gap, intrepidly proclaiming aloud that "greater is HE that is in ME than he who is in the world!" It was an awesome shift in my spiritual life and I felt HIS POWER flowing in and through the prayer.

The next day, I called her, the pastor's wife, telling my friend that they must be up against something very BIG for me to have received such a strong push back from the spiritual realm! She confirmed my impression with what *she* had received in prayer, and we agreed to stand together in Christ.

That afternoon, driving home after an errand I passed a woman on the street corner holding a sign: CANCER × 3, DESPERATE, PLEASE HELP! I drove by. A block farther, I heard internally: "Stop and go back" and argued with the thought (someone else will stop) and went on. Another block passed, and again I felt prompted to go back, and again I resisted. The third prompt was very specific: "TURN AROUND HERE!" and I finally obeyed, turned around, drove back, and pulled into the parking lot behind her.

I called her over to my car. We talked about why she was there, what her real needs were, and what she hoped to accomplish. We shared our individual cancer stories, held each other, and wept. I gave her what I was prompted to give, and she burst into tears a second time as I handed it to her. It was a sacred, humbling moment, and I was awash with JESUS loving her through me. We embraced again, and I gave her a tender kiss on the cheek from Jesus before I drove away with tears streaming down my face.

As I neared home, I was prompted to turn into the local church parking lot—and *this* time, I obeyed immediately. I walked into the building and found the halls dark and the pastor's door closed. I turned to walk away but heard internally, "Knock" (I did) and the reverend's voice unexpectedly invited me to enter! With a big smile, I told him that I guessed God wanted me to deliver a big hug from HIM and embraced him with a holy hug. I asked if his wife had shared my prayer experience with him. The answer was "Yes."

He excitedly told me of how during the midst of a heated discussion with the church board members, they had shared my experience of "push back" with them as the conflict escalated, which not only stopped the conflict and reunified the group, but drove the lone dissenter to leave permanently! They all agreed afterward, if the attack was this overt and nasty, there must be a great work coming and they wanted to be unified IN GOD and no longer yielding to dissension and division!

I was learning that Your children Lord are everywhere, and so is the adversary!

After all I had seen and experienced, I knew I would not ever give up the JESUS I found in the Mass or His sweet presence in the Eucharist. But I loved seeing Him in the churches I was visiting. I loved sharing Him across all denominational borders and seeing Him so clearly in those people and places—as well as being surprised by souls standing on street corners. This funny, kind, loving, surprising, magnanimous GOD was beginning to fill out my understanding.

All the story pieces were beginning to fall together into an image I could adore and love without fully comprehending or understanding; the fact that HE KEPT SHOWING UP was becoming sufficient for me.

Chapter 22

The Confrontation

It was on Easter Sunday that a woman came forward at the little local church to speak to us and let us know that she had been praying for my brother. She shared her story with us, telling us that she had been diagnosed schizophrenic and institutionalized for four years as a younger woman. A visiting pastor had discerned her issue as being more spiritual than physical and asked for permission to pray over her. For many years, she had felt that was the case, and was so relieved that this man saw and believed her, that she readily granted him permission. He summarily prayed exorcism prayers over her commanding the demonic forces to leave, refusing to leave until *they* did—and they DID. She was FREE. She was released two weeks later.

Knowing my brother's story, this beautiful soul offered to pray for my brother if I would stand in for him. I did. She prayed. Her prayer was powerful, authoritative, and Spirit-led as she commanded that which was tormenting my brother to LEAVE and thanked "Father GOD" for the healing that would be made manifest in him! I wept openly. John was deeply touched, and both of us felt the atmosphere shift, like a heavy blanket enveloping and then being pulled off, something had happened.

We went home truly *expecting* to see a change in my brother, but we did not see him that day at all. He had been sequestered in his quarters since Friday. He came out three days later on Easter Monday. The miracle was undeniable. It was my brother, the one I had never before seen, even in childhood. No longer wrapped up in dark thoughts or paranoia, there was a distinct lightness and joy I had never felt around him before. He laughed, he played, he stayed in our presence for hours, enjoying us and allowing us to enjoy him.

He joined us for every meal, we played games and talked for hours. We washed dishes together, told jokes, and one afternoon that precious week, while running errands, he actually called to tell me that he LOVED me. He didn't want or need anything; there was no other reason for the call, he just wanted to connect and tell me that I was loved! I fell in love with this funny sweet man that was my brother and praised GOD for His goodness! Unfortunately, I was not aware of the spiritual rules that go with a healing of this nature. When ill spirits are driven out—they must be replaced with the Holy Spirit, and the soul strengthened to resist their efforts to return. We were so delighted with this new version of my brother, yet it never occurred to either of us to *tell* him what had happened or *why he was free!*

The morning of the seventh day, I went to his room to greet him, excited about the prospect of sharing another day with this new beloved brother to be rebuffed by a guttural growling: "What do YOU want?!"

Totally caught off guard, I responded carefully, "To wish you good morning."

"Yeah, right!"

I asked if he was okay, and he snapped, "No, I'm *not* okay!"

I leaned in and asked what had happened, and he growled back, "You know what happened, the same thing that *always* happens!"

The ugliness in this voice was palpable, so unlike what I had heard the past six days and I longed to have "my brother" back. I felt my heart begin to beat wildly in anticipation of the battle to come. Normally, I would have responded in anger to the ill spirit that had seemingly taken hold, but deep in my spirit resounded the cry "I will *not* let his Easter healing go so easily!"

Instead, I steadied with the extraordinary grace being made available by the Holy Spirit, gently submitted that nothing had changed, and asked why he was so upset. A long laundry list of past imagined grievances spewed forth with an unholy rush of anger and hatred. I gently chided, saying those things were not true—then called to him—to the brother I knew was in there, asking him did he not remember the joy and peace of the last six days?

"Do you not remember your EASTER?"

There was a pause, his eyes and voice cleared momentarily as he looked directly at me and wistfully said, "Yes." He DID remember. His face softened for a moment as he reflected that yes, Easter had been wonderful—but that was THEN and this was NOW, and the malevolence raised its head once more. Again, I gently chided and invited him to come back into the present with me where there was love and happiness and peace. I tried to wrap around his spirit with my voice, speaking softly and lovingly.

"Choose to stay with me now. Choose to have another good day. JUST START TODAY OVER."

To my great surprise, the expression on his face again changed, his voice became light, and he stood up, held out his hand to shake mine and delightedly crowed, "IT'S A DEAL!"

And then we had tea. AMAZING.

I had won the skirmish, but later in the week, the battle would resume, and the forces we would face were MUCH bigger! I watched his spirit struggle, as the darkness overcame him once again and the ugliness returned full force, commanding me to "GET OUT!" when I came to greet him. Those sweet miraculous Easter days were the last time I "saw" my brother unencumbered by darkness.

Unfortunately, the spirits that came back brought friends. BIG ONES. He never again came out of his room to socialize or "be" with us despite my many invitations. He became convinced my husband was trying to kill him, and that we were putting poisonous "dust" through his ventilation system in his room. We hired someone to come check the ducts and even *their* assurance that they were clean was not enough. It was a hot, dry summer, and his room was indeed "dusty" with no real explanation of where it was coming from. He taped up every duct, and yet there was still dust.

His rooms were locked (we did not even HAVE a key), yet he was convinced that we were breaking in. As his paranoia increased, we started locking our bedroom door at night out of fear. He began hoarding water and eating only in his room. As things escalated, I would stand outside his door quietly, praying for him.

One night, I heard him in "conversation" with these dark entities—in Chinese of all things. As far as I know, my brother does not speak the language, though he does know some phrases that he learned from a man that was in the rehab program with him in Baltimore. This was very different. The dialogue was dark and ugly-sounding, and my brother's responses were disquieting. I went to my room and got a vial of oil a priest friend had given me that he had blessed with an exorcism prayer and made a small sign of the cross on his door.

Immediately, I heard raging, things being thrown, yells of protest, then a demonic sounding laugh. I kept praying but to no avail. I finally went back to my room, not knowing what to do against something so BIG that it *laughed* at my prayers! At this point in my life, I had very little understanding of the demonic realm, and what we do not understand we are helpless to stand against. I would love to write that I figured it all out, rebuked the evil that was attacking my brother (and us through him), but that was not the case. It would be many years before I learned about the forces we were up against.

The next morning, I stood before my brother's door and timidly called out to him, "Are you okay?"

An ugly voice snarled back, "As if *you* care!"

I gently persisted, "Of course I care—*I LOVE YOU!*—I just want you to be all right."

The response was cryptic, malicious sounding: *"Oh yes, I am good now. You will see before the day is over. They are coming."*

What we didn't know was that after I had anointed his door with blessed oil, the angry demonic forces spoke into him, and he called the Department of Human Services telling them that we had poured foul smelling oil throughout his rooms. He told them we were verbally abusive, putting toxic dust down his ductwork, and that my husband was trying to kill him. The holy oil had certainly had "an effect" on the demonic forces tormenting him—just not the one I had hoped for!

The investigation started immediately. Friends and family were interviewed. We were blessed to have a discerning investigator who saw clearly through the demonic smokescreen, and what could have become an even greater nightmare was circumvented. He came to us, after talking to everyone else, asked us to sit down, and soberly laid all the cards on the table.

"Your brother is mentally unstable and at this point, dangerous. You need to get him out of your house, or he *will* hurt you."

I remember my panicked response well: "We CAN'T kick him out! He'll die!"

And his sobering reply of "No. He won't. They almost never do. But you or your husband *will.* You must move him out." He shook our hands as he left and wished us well.

Investigation closed.

We began to search out alternatives to housing and found out there were none. The waiting list for Section 8 housing was three years, and he had to be homeless to be put on that list. Not an option. Rents were too high to put him in his own house. We were stymied.

Again, GOD was already working on the problem.

My brother had made an online friend during an episode of trying to quit smoking, and they had stayed in touch. His online persona was quite normal…kind…gentle. When he presented his case of "severe abuse" to her and her husband, they believed every word and rapidly implemented a plan to rescue him. The husband arrived at our home from the west coast with a U-HAUL trailer and silently packed my brother up as I watched, my heart breaking. He refused to talk to us, and the ugliness raging in my brother refused to acknowledge my tears or hear my declaration of love for him. They drove away, both of their faces set like flint, sullen and determined. It was a sad day for me, though after the angst and tears that came with watching them drive away, there *was* a measure of relief mixed with the pain. Perhaps he would find peace in this new life that he was choosing. Perhaps GOD had answered our prayers in a very unconventional way.

Once they arrived, he immediately plugged into the system there, and his "stories of abuse" gave him a leg up into the system.

He was able to get help there that I could not get for him here. What had taken me years to accomplish here, was orchestrated in mere weeks there.

Five months later, I got an angry call from my brother's rescuer: "Your brother is totally crazy! I have taken him to a hotel and paid for his first week there—after that he is YOUR problem!"

Apparently, in a fugue state my brother had cut all the buttons off of his clothes and then accused the man's wife of the "crime" threatening retribution if she ever did something like that to him again. Her husband, finally realizing that they had deeply misread the situation, got him out of their home and called me. The beautiful part is that GOD used the gift that this couple had given and turned it into a miracle provision for my brother.

A few weeks later, housing came through for my brother, and he was embraced by the system in place there. He had a tough time in the beginning as he battled with the demons that had brought him there, but with persistence and effort on his part, things began to settle down and he began to create a life for himself. People look down on those that struggle with mental illness assuming that somehow "they are weak," "less than." My experience is that quite the opposite is true. They withstand voices and perceived "realities" that many other souls would give up and fold under. My brother has never quit. And GOD has never quit looking after him. First through me and my husband, then via his rescuers, and now through the system designed for those like him.

GOD IS INDEED GOOD. HE DID WHAT I COULD NOT.

The lovely part is that I have never forgotten the brother I met that EASTER and the great LOVE I had (and still have) for him. I know that "he" is there inside him, bravely battling the forces that come against him daily. He recently told me that the big demonic forces did not follow him to the hotel that day, and though he has endured ups and downs, his mind has distinct periods of clearness, and he IS HAPPY.

His move ended our twenty-year saga, and it became evident it would take time for me and John to heal from the hurts of so many years of familial dysfunction. So much of our marriage and lives together had been wrapped up in my brother's presence in our lives and his pain. As I healed, I began to treasure all that I had learned on the journey. Good thing too—GOD was about to turn my world upside down again, and I would need everything that I had learned for the next part of the story.

It was a confirmation year, and that Christmas, one of my confirmands came to me with a desperate plea to go to the hospital and pray for her mother who had just been diagnosed with terminal cancer. I went. I prayed for her mother, but there were no messages from heaven, no signs to bring solace to the daughter's grieving heart. Two weeks later, I heard that her mom was not doing well and felt a distinct prompting to go back up to the hospital.

On my arrival to her room, I found her laying on a temperature-monitoring system that digitally declared her temperature at the foot of her bed. Her husband informed me she had been fighting high fevers that the doctors couldn't seem to knock back. The monitor read 103.8. She was moaning and thrashing in her bed in great discomfort, unresponsive to our presence. I invited the husband to take a break and grab a cup of coffee in the cafeteria while I took over the "watch," and he gratefully accepted.

The moment he left the room, I heard GOD say, "*STAND UP. RAISE YOUR HANDS AND COMMAND THEM TO STOP TORMENTING MY DAUGHTER AND LEAVE!*"

I had never heard or done anything like that before, but I *had* seen it modeled at Powerhouse Church, and I understood what GOD was asking me to do. Since I was now alone, I felt I could *do* what I'd been asked and stood up, raised my hands, and commanded the tormenting spirits of fever to LEAVE! NOW! In the NAME of JESUS CHRIST! They were no longer to be permitted to torment the Lord's daughter.

As I prayed, I watched the digital display at the foot of the bed change. Within moments, 103.8 became 103.6, then 103.4, then 103.2, then 103. I watched, my eyes widening, incredulous at the steady movement downward; 103 became 102.8. I looked to the side and realized the husband had reentered—startled, suddenly self-conscious—I apologized and stopped praying.

He cried out, "No, don't stop! I see what is happening!" But the downward movement had been broken and the temperature remained at 102.8. The beauty of the moment was that her temperature never again went up over that, and she rested peacefully from that point on until she passed from this life into the next!

Driving home, I marveled at what had just happened, and reasoned that when you *do* what GOD *tells* you to do—HE ACTS. There had been a storm raging in this woman's body, and HE had stilled the storm.

Chapter 23

The Push

With my brother gone, we had no need of a big house and decided to sell. My mentor friend was in the process of rebuilding a rescued house in another town and offered to rent it to us. The drive seemed daunting, but there was something about the house that beckoned, and we began to make plans. It was May again (tornado month) and storms were on the horizon as we went to bed.

John fell straight asleep. I stayed up to pray.

All of a sudden, I felt a lowering over our house that instinctively I knew was not good, and I got out of bed and prayed against it until it lifted moments later. The next morning, we awoke to damage and fences down throughout our neighborhood and reports of a tornado several miles away. The interesting part was *ours* was the only fence left standing and we had no damage whatsoever. It had begun to lower over our house, had lifted, and smashed down mere yards away. This was my first lesson in prayer in relation to weather events.

We downsized, moving forty minutes away to a small rural town. We went from 3,000 square feet to 1,200. So much "stuff" had to go. To make the transition even more difficult, the new house had no cupboards, or closets—and limited shelving—meaning, we would have to rethink where everything we *had* kept would go. It was an interesting time in our lives. I was still leading the youth ministry, and despite all the tumult and chaos, it was our best year ever. The team worked together well, teens had been touched and changed, "i's had been dotted and t's had been crossed."

The end of the year found me exhausted and weary but satisfied that we had "done well." I approached the pastor about the church sending me on a restorative retreat to heal my aching spirit and was shocked by his retort: "What have you done that deserves THAT?" I was crushed. I had literally poured myself out into the program over many hours (and years) and he even questioned whether I had earned the stipend they paid me, asking for a breakdown of time spent and work done! Dismissively, he noted, "I've not heard anything bad about you, but I haven't heard anything good either." That was the arrow that pierced my heart, and I hung up the phone and wept.

A few days later, I tendered my resignation.

The irony is that I had NO idea what GOD was doing—I saw only the cold lack of appreciation for over ten years of giving everything I had, as imperfect as the offering was. I did not realize that my pastor was being "used" to get me into the spot GOD wanted me to serve in and to set me up for the next step of my journey after that! I have always been deeply loyal and committed, and had he not done what he had done, I'd be there still. I had not yet learned to move freely when called. I had to be pushed out of the nest before I learned to spread my wings and fly!

I felt pushed out of my job, and deeply hurt, not yet understanding the "whys" behind it all. I remember crying out to JESUS that I did not understand how my life's work could mean so little and be dismissed so easily! I actually felt him smile softly and shake his head saying *that* was *not* your life's work—merely *training* for what is to come! Shocked, I wondered what that comment could possibly mean. It snapped me out of my pity party mind-set and got me looking for where I was to serve next. We found a little country church a mere three blocks away from our new home and checked in!

One Sunday, the scheduled lector did not show up and I offered to fill the position. Reading the Word is my gift, and the spirit flows through the proclamation. The pastor there was generous of spirit, and cleverly put me in charge of training their Lectors, which meant immediate integration into the parish. The next year, I volunteered to teach, and I taught four years in their Religious Education program.

I will never forget my last two years there and the young people that joined me in seeking out the presence of JESUS! It was an amazing, sweet intimate time as instead of being in a room of sixty-plus I had between ten and fourteen. It was lovely and often intense as we connected deeply with JESUS and each other. It was with those young people I learned to invite JESUS into the room, and He would show up and interact with each one individually during a meditative prayer experience. The sacredness and authenticity of the experience was undeniable as each shared their individual encounters with Him; it was an amazing time in my life and in theirs. Their names are still written in my prayer logs, and I remember them often in my prayer times as I thank Father GOD for His great goodness to me and to them!

Chapter 24

Speaking against the Storms

It was during this time that God began "schooling me" on His power over storms. I'd already seen His authority over a physical storm in one of his children when He stopped the advance of a fever, causing torment and distress by asking me to raise my hands and declare to the spirits to STOP in HIS NAME. I still had not quite wrapped my head around what had happened, only that if I did what HE asked, HE would act. It was enough for the moment.

I had tried praying over the sick since then with weak results and decided that perhaps it was my medical background that hindered rather than helped. Knowing all the "impossibilities" even though I had once been healed myself, somehow affected my faith and understanding of this GOD OF THE IMPOSSIBLE, and I found myself defaulting to "thy will be done" not knowing quite how "to open" the spiritual doors that bring His will to manifest in the kingdom. I still did not understand what He was trying to show me.

The first spring storm after we moved was on May 31, 2013. It was the biggest tornado to hit the state ever. We were no longer living in "tornado alley central," yet here we were facing another monster. As close as the other storms came, this was the first time I was ever afraid. We sought shelter with our dogs in our landlord's basement and prayed. It was a wicked, treacherous storm that spawned ugly multiple twisters, coming down like octopi arms out of the sky. The storm was indeed a monster: 2.6 miles wide, the largest tornado ever measured on Earth.

It was also incredibly violent, and though it packed winds as high as 296 mph (higher than any measured EF-5) because of the way the Fujita scale is based on the damage left behind, it was officially only rated a strong EF-3. Too much of the tornado occurred over unpopulated areas to rate it higher despite the size and wind speed. It took the lives of eight people, all of whom died in vehicles. What affected me most was the evil character of the storm. Truly malevolent. I understood for the first time that GOD was not an accomplice in this destruction. Just as He was not a part of the fever that had been tormenting his daughter in the hospital. Pieces of the puzzle were beginning to fall together.

That was not the last big storm to hit, as we were double-whammied two years later by horrendous ice storms in December of 2015. It was two years later that JESUS began schooling me on *who* I was *IN HIM and what that meant in the spiritual realm.* He spoke into me the realization that if I believed that the Holy Spirit truly dwelled in me—and that the Father Son and Holy Spirit are truly three-in-one—*then HE WAS PRESENT in me as well.*

I began to ask unabashedly to be clothed in His righteousness, to step into my true identity as a daughter of the most high God. I read the Word daily, went to Mass often, prayed rosary after rosary seeking Him.

One day, as I sat on my porch in the morning sunshine, kissed by sweet breezes, watching the elms across the street dance with each other, branches swaying in the wind; I was overcome by His presence. Then in a moment of boldness, I asked Him to send me a sign.

I asked for a bird to land on the railing two feet in front of me as a signal that he was feeling *me* love HIM too!

Imagine my surprise, when immediately a bright blue Jay flew from across the street and landed directly in front of me, cocking his little head, surveying me, tail bobbing up and down. As I marveled, studying his lovely plumage, a brilliant red Cardinal, black-faced, crest-raised, joined him! Both of them paused, as if waiting for me to be certain they were there "for me" before flying off at the exact same moment. Never before in all my prayer times outside had a bird ever graced my porch, much less TWO at once! I knew JESUS was feeling my love for Him as surely as I was feeling Him loving ME!

I Googled the significance of seeing a blue jay: The significance of seeing a cardinal.

Both are believed to be a sign from God.

Hmmm.

I began earnestly praying before each Mass that He would cover me in His righteousness and that I would be able to stand before the throne worthily. One Sunday, I worded my request a little differently and found out just how carefully our LORD listens to our requests. Kneeling, I asked for JESUS to wrap me in HIS ROBE OF RIGHTEOUS-NESS, to which I heard internally his immediate response: (*Feeling a gentle smile in his voice*) "WOULD YOU LIKE THE ERMINE ONE?"

I looked up startled, saw nothing out of the ordinary, but, certain of the voice, replied with a soft "Yes." It was cold that morning, and a warm fur robe would be welcome! Immediately, I felt a warm enfolding softness wrap completely around me. It was an exquisite sensation, and the PEACE and LOVE that came with it, undeniable. I snuggled into its richness, amazed that JESUS would offer such a sweet and sacred gift to honor my request!

The next week, my classes in storm management with JESUS began.

I was sitting in the living room of our little house watching the afternoon news when I saw a weather report forecasting a strong storm coming our way! A twinge of fear engendered by a history of so many violent storms had me listening intently. Suddenly, I became aware of another voice. It was firm, steady, and instructive. The same voice I had heard in the hospital.

"GO OUTSIDE. RAISE YOUR HANDS AND COMMAND IT TO GO AROUND!"

I was home alone; there was no one around outside as everyone had hunkered down for the impending storm, so like I had in the hospital, I felt I could *do* what was being asked and walked outside onto the porch. The sky was dark, the wind had picked up, and the smell of rain was in the air. The TV radar had shown us directly in the oncoming path of the storm and my view confirmed what I'd seen and heard. I raised my hands, faced the storm and commanded it to GO AROUND in the name of JESUS CHRIST, and then retreated back inside. Imagine my surprise when the storm went around our little town leaving us dry and undamaged by the winds!

WOW! DID THAT JUST HAPPEN!?

John came home from work shortly after, and I excitedly shared with him what had occurred. His response? A lifted eyebrow, a head-shake, and the declaration that despite appearances, it was just coincidence. Internally, I knew otherwise (after all, I had *heard* the voice clearly), but it was hard to be disbelieved by the one who knew me best. Interestingly enough, it happened again. And again. And again. By the fourth time, he acknowledged that *something* was going on that could not be explained in the natural.

Every time a severe manifestation of weather was called for—I would speak out against it—commanding it to go around in the authority of the Christ present within me, in HIS HOLY NAME! And each time IT DID. For a total of seventeen times, with the seventeenth time being the most spectacular (and documented). Interestingly enough, the number 17 in Hebrew is *Yod Zayin*, which also means victory, and is a symbol of spiritual weaponry. I had spoken with a pastor friend of mine in the city, seeking deeper understanding, and he had counseled to just keep doing what I was doing and see where the LORD was leading me with it. Number 17 was indeed a victory and a sign of spiritual weaponry.

I was watching an afternoon show on TV when a weather alert popped up on the screen with a strong warning: Straight-line winds of 60 to 70 mph were going through two nearby towns, heading for ours, and all in the path of this storm needed to prepare immediately. Sitting on my couch, all of a sudden I thought to myself, *Hell, no! You are not coming here!* and I rushed outside to pray against it! Raising my hands in the direction of the impending winds, I commanded them by the authority given to me by the CHRIST within me TO GO AROUND OR STOP at our city limits—it would NOT be permitted to enter!

As I sat back down on my couch, the weatherman again appeared with quite a bemused look on his face saying that he had no idea *why*—but the incoming winds had literally dropped from 70 to a mere 40 mph at our city limits! The seventeenth time was indeed a victory! I laughed out loud PRAISING GOD in His goodness, and a moment later, my phone rang. It was my pastor friend; and he, too, was laughing! Almost chortling, he declared, "That was YOU, wasn't it?" Together we rejoiced, but I had yet to understand the *why* of it all. It would not be until we made our move to the northeast, that the pieces would all fall into place.

A prophetic painting class was offered on the outskirts of a nearby city, and I was compelled by a friend to attend. The cover of this book is the result of the first class I attended. A pastor prayed over us before we began our assigned project (to paint a cross), and he perused me carefully as he prayed. Coming down from the little stage area he walked over to me and said, "I see a large chrysalis over you, open, releasing a large butterfly. Paint what you see."

Much to the chagrin of the instructor who was leading the group in the execution of a cross, I began painting what I was seeing in my head: a soul, hands lifted, Holy Spirit overhead, pouring grace down, swirling around, lifting up, lining up mind and heart with the mind and heart of Christ, Holy Spirit fire falling all around! The painting was not my style, the subject matter not my design, but it flowed as easily from my brushes as anything I had ever created.

I left the class, wet painting and supplies in hand, unable to even open the door to let myself out without assistance. As I got close to my car, I realized that I would not be able to get in without putting something down, and I began to worry about how I would manage. At that moment, a tall emaciated homeless man with long scraggly hair walking through the parking lot to a nearby camp, noted my quandary and offered to assist. Not wanting to take any chances with the still wet painting, I looked at my options, AND HANDED HIM MY PURSE! The surprise on his face was clear as he looked at my face, looked at the purse in his hands, and then back at the camp. Oblivious, I opened the trunk of my car, safely stowed the painting and gear and then turned to thank him for holding my purse for me. (I realized at that moment that giving a stranger a bag holding all my valuables had probably not been the wisest choice!) I looked him in the eye gratefully; he nodded, *smiled the BIGGEST smile*, handed me my purse, and then turned to go back to the homeless camp. As he walked away, I watched his back straighten, his shoulders square, and his pace quicken. *Our thoughts mirrored one another's: "What was she (I) thinking? I handed him my purse...she trusted me with her purse!"* All of a sudden, he exploded in the JOY of being seen as a trustworthy person and began SKIPPING! He skipped across the road, a field, and all the way into the invisible camp hidden under the trees, and as he skipped, my heart did too. It was a crazy, lovely, powerful moment for BOTH of us.

That last summer wove around an extraordinary experience as I was slowly drawn into taking care of three feral cats. An apprehensive black mama and two hissy steel-gray kittens appeared on our covered porch the winter before seeking respite from the intense cold. We provided an insulated cardboard box to curl up in and a heated water bowl and food. They were grateful and showed their gratitude with great fecundity!

Those three untouchable felines multiplied in the spring and summer months, producing SIXTEEN kittens—litter after litter showing up on my porch! I dutifully provided bedding, food, and water and captured, spayed, and neutered the babies. Our breakfast room became a dedicated postsurgery "recovery room" much to my husband's chagrin. Our front porch became a giant nursery for all the mamas and their babies.

It was a lovely, relaxed time for all of them. Nothing to run from, no food to search out. The babies quickly accepted my presence, playing around my feet with the occasional brave one climbing into my lap to be petted and loved on. I enjoyed many an evening with sweet babies in my lap, mamas laying close by trusting my "watch," and the big male tomcat overseeing all from the top stair. They each had names; they all were loved and appreciated as individuals.

Try as I might, I only found homes for six kittens, leaving me with fourteen cats counting adults. THAT IS A LOT OF CATS. We would come home, and cats would literally flow from every corner up and over the porch—a sleek river of multicolored felines meowing for their dinner! A few were intrepid and terribly brave, allowing us to pick them up and carry them. Three were terribly timid, avoiding all contact, and the rest were comfortably weaving in and out of our feet granting "nose kisses." How I loved that summer of cats!

But God was about to move again.

Everything was about to change. Doors would close. Days would darken. Windows would open just as we thought there were no more options. In a surprise turn of events, we were assigned a new priest. It was a difficult transition for all. We all struggled to find new footing, but the changes came fast, and by the end of the year he had closed down the Religious Education Program. The door there slammed shut.

That December, a horrible virus blew through the town killing almost all of the cats. I lost a cat a day for ten days. Only four survived. I was devastated. Mourning their loss, I felt that the money I had spent spaying, neutering, giving shots, buying cages and food had all been wasted, the time and effort all *wasted*, and I was disconsolate. Crying out to God, I suddenly heard a calm, comforting voice softly asked, "*Did you have a good summer? Did the kitties have a good summer? They were relaxed and happy with none of the usual feral cat fears.* you *gave them that, and you saved* six. it was worth it all."

The next day, a dozen red roses were delivered to my front door, sent by Chewy (the food delivery service I had used) offering a sweet note of solace. It felt like God had gently finished closing the door that had been so painfully slamming shut. I sat head in hands and wept.

Two doors had closed and with them the stress in our household had magnified. John was unhappy in his job, broken-hearted over the cats, and we had lost three dogs over the past year in a trifecta of old age, sickness, and accident. We were done. We were disconnected from each other holding on to our own sorrows and heartache. It was a cold, disconsolate winter.

Out of the blue, John got a job offer up north. Full-time travel. Living in hotels. Great pay, benefits, and per diem. The catch? He had to leave in two weeks! I looked at our little house seeing my wall of plants, remaining cats and so much stuff—quickly declared such a quick move impossible—and he declined the offer on a Friday.

The irony was, the second he declined, I had second thoughts and began to feel sick inside... somehow "knowing" that "no" had been the *wrong* answer. There was the distinct feeling that GOD was opening this window to save us, and we had refused and slammed it shut again. Perhaps there was a reason for the new priest closing the RE classes down, a reason we had lost so many animals so quickly. A reason we were so unhappy now. Perhaps all the doors had been closed so we could move, so we *would* move.

GOD WAS PUSHING US OUT AGAIN.

Interestingly enough, that Monday he received a personal call from the person that would become his new boss. They talked a long time. The company was extending the consideration window to allow us time to process the idea. He was the man for the job, and they wanted him to reconsider! This time I made phone calls (checking with our landlord, asking about subletting, finding homes for plants and the two remaining kittens) and as all the pieces fell easily into place, we found ourselves saying yes. Yes, to change, yes to downsizing yet again, yes to God.

GOD WAS TELLING US TO JUMP.

A month later, John was on his way, and I was left to pack up and finish making all the necessary arrangements. GOD sent a sub-letter that was happy to lease the house for a year at a reduced rate in exchange for allowing my personal belongings and furnishings to remain intact.

It was the perfect arrangement. I didn't have to sort, pack, make all the "keep"/"give away" decisions or put things into storage.

A dear friend had just moved into a home with a large Florida room that easily embraced all my plants, and the perfect home came out of nowhere for the two indoor kittens I had rescued from the plague's onslaught. I literally just cleaned, cleared space for our new renter's personal belongings, packed what I wanted to bring in my car, and LEFT.

No severe weather had touched our little town since I began covering it in prayer the last two years we lived there. As I drove away, I encircled my beloved town with a blessing asking GOD to continue to protect her. A little over a month later, on Saturday, May 25, a tornado destroyed a mobile home park, hotel, and car dealership on the outskirts of town, stopping short at the sign that declared: Welcome to Our City.

Coincidence?

Mere days before that, on May 20, a historic setup for a cataclysmic tornadic event presented for Oklahoma City and the surrounding area. The potential for multiple violent tornadoes was terrifying, and meteorologists stressed the extreme nature of the threat as schools closed and shops shuttered their doors in anticipation of the outbreak. It was carried on national news feeds, and I watched the computer models in horror. I went online and found a predictive voice I trusted and wrote down what he said had to happen (and not happen) for this event to actually occur. Then I started praying.

If I was afraid all the way up here, I could only imagine what the people in Oklahoma were feeling! Suddenly, I had an epiphany! Contact every prayer warrior I knew, teach them how to pray against the oncoming onslaught and stop the mega-event en-masse! I sent out hundreds of instructive emails and texts challenging souls to stand up to this evil manifestation and PRAY—and PRAY THEY DID. Many did exactly as asked—standing on porches throughout the city commanding the storm to stand down, using the language provided by the meteorologist to speak against what needed to happen for the event to occur.

Was there a storm? Yes. Were there tornadoes? Yes. But nothing of the magnitude that had been predicted. No deaths. No horrific damage. Meteorologists came on Twitter calling it the event that didn't happen, saying they had absolutely NO idea why.

But we did.

Every soul that had stood the gap and prayed on their porches resolutely in the face of the storm on May 20—and rejoiced in the outcome on May 21.

I had my answer. That storm—the one that *didn't* happen—was the reason He taught me to pray the way He did so I could teach others the day they needed it.

Chapter 25

Home 2

One dog had survived that terrible year of death and affliction. A cheeky little gray Schnauzer girl. I had rescued her, emaciated and covered with ticks, from the side of the road years before; but she was 100% JOHN'S DOG. Her steady nonverbal love for him had given him something I could not—silent unconditional acceptance. She was the one that could not, would not, be given away, or left behind. Together, she and I drove away into a future that no one could foresee.

It was a long three-day journey and we arrived exhausted to our new "home." The next six months were spent residing in a Hilton Hotel called ironically Home 2. The staff quickly became family, our little girl dog the resident diva, and I fell into a new routine of minimalist living, packing up and going wherever my husband's company decided to send him, for however long they wanted, always coming back to our Home 2 family. It was like being on vacation.

Until it wasn't.

At around mid-August, John got a nasty-looking tick bite that just didn't heal. Instead of alarm bells going off in my head as a Lyme disease survivor, I brushed it off. Until he got SICK. Very, VERY SICK. His timing was impeccable. The company that had brought him onboard lost the new contract, and all of a sudden, his job was in jeopardy. The new company was convinced by his boss to move him over, and he got a new job description AND a raise with one big caveat: We would no longer be provided housing. We had to live on the economy, and housing costs were HIGH.

We had just received this news when he got sick. So sick he could not stand. So sick that he lay on the floor, crying, the pain untouched by the painkillers that had been prescribed. It took a trip to the ER to figure out that it was tick-bite related and treatment to begin and another trip to stop the train-wreck that was happening inside him as his body crashed. Secondary infections, an accompanying high fever and inflammation were wreaking havoc and he thrashed in agony as the medical personnel scurried to start IVs, dose meds, and run tests.

Our loyal Home 2 family looked after Sasha, our beloved dog, as I stayed by John's side that night in the ER, praying for God to intervene and spare his life. After a large dose of steroids, morphine, and anti-inflammatories, he finally rested; and I cried out to GOD in my distress and panic. Here we were in a strange place, in-between jobs, and my husband was in danger of dying! I had followed every prompting, left everything and everyone I loved behind to do so, and I challenged GOD saying, "You CANNOT just leave me a widow, living out of my car on the side of the road after all this! I NEED YOU TO *DO* SOMETHING!"

Almost immediately, John took a turn for the better, and instead of being admitted, he was sent home. I had my MIRACLE.

Two days later, we went to Mass to thank GOD for his goodness toward us, and afterward John wanted to drive back. He was still weakened by his time fighting the tick-borne invaders, but as the hotel was close, I shrugged and acquiesced. Pulling out he turned the wrong way, but I assumed he was taking us out to lunch and remained silent until we were well out of town and past all the restaurants I knew of in the area. When I finally asked where he was going, the answer was quite unexpected—to an RV dealer two towns up the road! I protested, offering that it was Sunday, and that they were closed AND we had been there a week ago and already knew what they had. He persisted, and I let it go.

Another ten minutes up the highway, we passed a coach RV with a FOR SALE sign in the front windshield. He hit the brakes, did a quick turnaround, and we pulled in front of our soon-to-be new home. The owner showed up to give us a tour, and John was quite taken with the unit. Me, not so much. It seemed dark, small, and musty. I almost nixed the deal.

Thank God I didn't.

It was none of those things. My perception was being affected by an outside force that I still could not see or understand fully. Purchase price was agreed on, money withdrawn and paid, and the best part of the deal yet to be revealed. The seller was about to become our new landlord, allowing us to park our new home on her property facing a river, a mere fifteen feet from the river's bank.

Every morning for the next three months, I woke up to "God TV." Blue herons and white egrets intently stalked the shallows. Slow spiraling ospreys soared high above encouraging their fledgling young on their first flights out of the nest, as I watched the living waters of the river ebb and flow at the command of the sea. Glorious shimmering blankets of diamonds that sparkled across the rippling currents coming in and going out left me in awe. God had responded to my heartfelt cries in an amazing show of goodness! If it weren't for the multitude of mosquitoes that swarmed up to eat us when we exited the coach to walk our little dog in the evenings, I would have considered it heaven!

Three months later, we were headed to Las Vegas on assignment, coach in storage, living in a Home 2 hotel at the edge of the Strip. It was a fun stay, and we enjoyed our time there checking out all the gourmet restaurants and extraordinary food. Little did we know that our world was about to be turned upside down once again in mere months. We had to let our little girl go on the drive back to our home at the end of February, her little doggie body was just done fighting.

We both felt the loss deeply, and our coach felt empty without her cheerful presence as we left "heaven" and pulled into the new RV park closer to John's work. We were now near the river instead of on; but we also had beaches, swimming pools, park expanses and wooded walking trails; not to mention an island community that welcomed us in. I felt like we had won the lottery!

That fall, John's older sister died, and we found ourselves headed west for a memorial service to celebrate her life. The flights were uneventful, and we arrived right on time at six thirty, disembarking to what we expected to be a good four-day visit with family. I went to the bathroom, and immediately my phone rang! It was John. His wallet was gone! He had taken it out of his pocket on the plane to pay for food and apparently not put it back securely!

We rushed back to the gate, but it was already locked. The good news was the plane was still there and was remaining in place for a ten-thirty flight! We found the Delta desk and told the young lady there our problem. She responded that there was absolutely *nothing* she could do and that we would have to check with lost-and-found tomorrow. With credit cards, all our money and his military ID inside the wallet; THAT was NOT an option.

If we left the airport, we would not be able to get back past security to fly home. CATCH-22. John began to panic. I began to rear up in the spirit and PRAY. I walked through the terminal praying aloud in tongues, convinced that the GOD who'd opened so many other doors in my life and moved storms could certainly get us back onto that plane to recover his wallet. Poor John did not know quite what to do with this version of his wife and left to go back to the gate in the hopes of catching the cleaning crew. I stopped and asked a security guard if it was possible to get the door opened, and they assured me it was possible that I just needed to get the right people involved.

Encouraged, I went back to the desk and engaged the young lady again. Again, she said, "Not possible." To which I responded gently but firmly, "Yes. I understand that it is not possible for *you* to open the door, but it *is* possible for SOMEONE to open the door, and I need you to call that person. That wallet contains essential documents and military IDs that must be recovered tonight. Make the call."

She did.

Amazingly, SHE could open the door. The key was hanging on the wall. She walked over to the gate, opened the door, went down into the plane, and found the maintenance crew working. She searched under the seats we'd been assigned and found nothing. She told the crew what she'd been looking for and left. Apologetically, she shook her head as she came through the door.

I asked her to go back again and recheck. She refused. I asked her to call the cleaning crew to see if they had found it. She called. They had not. At that point, I called upon the holy angels to get involved! Out loud, I asked them to push the wallet "right now" from wherever it had been hidden so that the maintenance crew would find it.

Minutes later, the phone rang. It was maintenance; they had found it IN THE AISLE *as they exited the plane!* Needless to say, I was exultant! In minutes, John had his wallet back! The trip was saved, we would not be sleeping in the airport; we *would* be going to his sister's celebration.

GOD HAD OPENED ANOTHER DOOR at my request, and the holy angels had heard and responded with a physical "push" to get the wallet back to us!

Chapter 26

A Protected Place

On March 2020, everything changed. COVID was front-page news, and images of body bags and reports of deaths in the thousands shocked everyone to the core. It was here. The government responded with lockdowns, masking, and a rush to develop a vaccine to "save humanity." It was an unnerving time, but we were in the best of all possible places. As they locked down all public venues and told people to isolate in "pods," we found ourselves in a large protected "pod" in the gated RV resort we were in. No one but residents being allowed in or out, we felt safe socializing together, gathering on the weekends in controlled groupings.

No one was exposed or caught the virus that spring or summer, and unlike so many others, we had a lovely time socializing with our new friends. We also connected with one of the island families, and once-a-week gatherings with that group of "COVID family" did much to keep us all sane.

Our favorite bar and grill was one of the last to close to dine in business and first to reopen. I was privileged to join their weekly musician there on stage for duets whenever he sang and played, which was a life-first for me, and we became good friends. An amazing musician, an engaging singer, and a generous teacher, I learned so much from him. I LOVED MY LIFE there.

Unfortunately, COVID was relentless, and John eventually brought it home from work on his way to Las Vegas, leaving me alone to face it in our coach, and he, alone in a hotel room in Vegas. I had never been so weak or so sick for so long, a full fourteen days of knock down illness, and another seven days before I really felt like I was finally in recovery mode.

My island family brought me everything I needed, delivered with a knock to the coach door, and monitored my recovery. John's family did the same for him in Las Vegas, bringing him food and water as the hotel would not allow in-room delivery.

Fear began to grip our nation, pushing it to agree to things that would have been unthinkable a mere six months earlier. Businesses were forced to close, people were forced to wear masks, and then mandatory vaccinations were enforced with the new mRNA vaccines still surrounded by warnings that were being erased and discounted. No one knew what to believe.

A New Tornado Zone

That spring, I found out something I'd not been aware of; our new location had TORNADOES! We were hearing reports of tornadic weather heading our way, and the RV resort had sent texts saying that we may be asked to evacuate. I had begun a daily online text ministry during the quarantine to encourage people with scripture and short teachings, and that morning, one of my grateful recipients had sent *me* a gift. A link to one of her favorite songs, and one that I had never heard before: "RAISE A HALLELUJAH!"

I listened to it (and the story behind the song) all of a sudden fully aware of what I was to do with it. I went outside in front of our coach, put the song on "play" and began to sing and pray along with the recording. I prayed against the coming storm, raising my hands, commanding it to go around our coach in the authority given to me as a daughter of the most-high God, praying over each tree around us (there were three) and commanding each to stand strong in the storm "in the name of JESUS" declaring that not a branch would be lost!

There was palpable power in this time of prayer, and when I was finished, I had a definitive sense of "It is done." The next morning when the storm hit in all its fury, John got up to watch. (He was still intending to go to work!) I lay in my bed and felt the entire unit begin to sway as the winds roared through and pictured myself in my heavenly Father's lap, being rocked back and forth like a small child. I was calm and totally at peace.

Suddenly, I heard John cry out, "Oh my gosh! You have GOT to see this!" Apparently, all the trees around us were being bent crazily by the wind, but the three trees that encircled us, inexplicably, were standing tall…not moving! The storm literally went around our little home! Not only did we not lose a branch, our trees did not even lose a LEAF!

Our yard was full of leaves whipped from the trees that lined the street, along with branches and litter from other yards, but not a single leaf from *our* trees! The fact that our trees had very distinctive leaves made the miracle easy to see and undeniable. All my potted plants were untouched. Sixty-eight old growth trees had come down, four units had been damaged (one totally crushed), and two vehicles destroyed. As we walked the RV park, we saw so much destruction everywhere. Only our yard was untouched.

It was at this point I shared my prestorm prayer vigil with my husband, and he understood that what he had seen our trees do that morning, had been exactly what I had commanded them (in the authority given to me by JESUS) to do.

I have struggled to figure out the final lesson in these storm events, endeavoring to link it to the possibility of praying more effectively for healing of physical storms that rage in people's bodies—guessing that perhaps since I know so little about the forces of nature it is easier for me to believe that GOD will MOVE weather than still a storm in a single body, which makes no sense at all! Still trying to figure that one out.

Chapter 27

The Carrot

People started shunning those who were not vaccinated even if they'd already had COVID. It was a bizarre time in our nation's history. After his bout with a tick-borne illness, John refused to be pushed into vaccination especially as we had both already *had COVID* and survived. His refusal cost him his job. An extremely generous offer from a big company down South inspired our move, a move made easy by the motorhome. We just battened down the hatches and drove away.

Five days later, we found ourselves in an asphalt RV park with a little strip of grass, mourning the loss of our beautiful RV resort and our friends. Our two years there was now just a treasured memory. The night we arrived, there was a huge storm and cyclo-bomb that hit within miles of us, shaking our coach and unnerving ME completely! I was not ready to do tornado weather in a motorhome!

The next day, I found a bigger, more protected RV park north and east of the city. When we called, they said there were no sites available and did not expect for there to be any for a couple of months. I felt a distinct prompting to drive to the premises, deciding as we pulled in that's where we wanted to live. PERIOD.

A beautiful lodge, bar and grill, laundry facilities, workout room, pool, fishing pond, and HUGE storm shelters sealed the deal for me. Silently, I told GOD he needed to get us in, and as we stood there, talking to the staff, a space opened up! It was a little too small (over the phone, they never would have offered it) our coach would barely fit along with one vehicle parked sideways. I would have to park at the front by the office, but I didn't care! Yes, yes, YES. We would take it! We moved in four days later. It was a good place to live, and I felt protected and loved by GOD as the site we were given was a mere sixty paces from the eighty-person storm shelter.

THANK YOU, PAPA!

We integrated quickly, finding ourselves close to all the local venues, and it became a time of healing and rest for both of us as we waited for the new job to process him in. We spent time connecting with family and friends. Imagine our surprise when the company reneged on their offer, leaving us to job hunt once again.

Four months later, out of the blue, came an offer from a state even farther south on the map. Never did I ever see us ending up that far south! I figured it was just a hotter, stormier version of where I had lived before and I had no desire to *go* there. But here it was. The job offer was solid. It would keep us within a four-hour driving distance for family visits. An important consideration, as God had been quietly working on my daughter's heart, and our relationship was now blossoming in a new and very beautiful way.

I found an RV park thirty minutes from his new job campus. WE WERE GOING.

I felt like GOD had tricked us into going south by stepping us through this first stop. He had dangled the big carrot to get us to move then pulled it away quickly leaving us sitting so that we would actually consider the next offer when it came.

Pretty slick, GOD! Pretty slick.

Chapter 28

The Arrival

We came in on a Saturday. The site was small. The grounds were barren, brown, and unimpressive. The community center was tiny, the facilities minimal after what we had been used to up north and at our last resort. I was NOT a happy camper. (Pun intended!)

On the third day there, I found myself in the entryway of the local Kroger grocery store in a close-by town, wondering what the heck just happened to our lives. Suddenly overcome, I burst into tears. Not pretty little drops sliding down rosy cheeks, but big, wet sobbing rivulets. A lady came out from behind the Starbucks counter, enquiring gently, hand on my shaking shoulder, "Are you okay?"

"No…no…I'm *not* okay!" slipped out between sobs, and she stood with me as I collected myself.

Her gentle kindness was not lost on me. In what world do absolute strangers do this?

Leaving the store, I asked GOD why He had brought us there. What possibly could be his plan? I implored Him to give me *something…anything* to hold onto! I had left everything behind three times now to follow where we felt He had been leading. I just needed a nod of some kind to let me know we were still on the right track.

Driving back toward the RV park, I passed a big sign that said: HISTORIC CITY CENTER and, on impulse, turned and parked in front of a furniture store. Getting out, squaring my shoulders, I walked in and asked, "Where's the owner?!" The man behind the counter laughed and replied that he was not there and that I would have to be satisfied with him! He was gracious and welcoming, and we talked for a long time as he gave me some history on the town and the people, encouraging me to walk up the block and check it out. I did.

I went into every storefront and found that most were self-owned and the people all equally welcoming as I shared my story. I got FIVE hugs as I made my way up Main Street, and two souls came out from behind their counters to pray over/with me that God would quickly make clear *why* I was there. I was overcome by this unsolicited welcome committee and a distinct feeling that after a lifetime of searching, I had finally found my "people," my tribe!

The discovery of a Catholic church at the end of the block was the cherry on the cake.

I HAD MY ANSWER.

One of my great affections is good espresso coffee. Our home on the water had been a proverbial "coffee desert," and I had missed my espressos dearly. This new city center, as small and rural as it was, actually had *choices*! From excellent espresso offerings in an upscale boutique to a hearty cup of café at a Mexican restaurant with a side of *migas*, to various coffee/espresso/tea offerings at a local nonprofit, there were so many choices! The nonprofit won my heart and soon became my regular stomping ground. In fact, I wrote most of this book sitting at their counter drinking cup after cup of coffee! I love the fact that it is managed by missionaries, and that the cheery staff will offer prayer upon request with your beverage of choice!

The Catholic church had been a wonderful discovery, and on that first day, I walked over to the office to check it out. The office was closed for lunch, but a Hispanic gentleman was walking toward the door from his car, and I engaged him in conversation. He offered to give me a tour of the facilities and church, and I gratefully accepted. We walked the grounds and entered the foyer, and as he explained the Church's history, he presented me with a packet with the full story to read later.

We walked toward the sanctuary's doors, and as he pulled the big door open, I was hit with a "wave of JESUS" that just about knocked me over! A look of astonishment washed over my face (I'd never experienced this entering a Catholic church before), and I looked him straight in the eye and declared firmly: "THANK you very much, but the tour is over! I just had an invitation from JESUS I cannot refuse!" He cocked his head slightly, smiled, and nodded, leaving me to enter and pray!

As I entered, I found the source of my JESUS wave of presence: A small group was in adoration before the monstrance in the small side chapel, and I knew I had my sign. This was where we were supposed to be. I WAS HOME.

The name of the church? The patron saint of miracles, patron saint of love, patron saint of lost things, patron saint of marriage, and surprisingly, the patron saint of animals.

Can you say full circle?

I quickly fell into a sweet daily routine of Mass, morning coffee at the nonprofit, and the occasional breakfast in town. As a surprise plus, my breakfast tab at the café was mysteriously picked up by an unidentified patron the first three times I went in after Mass! Apparently, not an unusual occurrence in this amazing little town.

My second week here, I requested permission to read at daily Mass and was permitted to enter the rotation—a great privilege, as proclaiming the Word into the hearts of the people is a singular joy for me. Soon after, I was introduced to a little humble Mexican priest assigned as vicar here, and he is the reason this book has come into being. Father listened to some of my story and encouraged me to sit and write the rest. An overwhelming endeavor, and in the beginning, I thought of it as having to "eat an elephant." But at his insistence, I just began by eating one bite at a time, starting "at the beginning."

As I wrote, I wondered what the purpose of this book would be and then realized that for each soul reading it the purpose would be different. Each soul would recognize a different door or window being opened and by virtue of their *own* stories pass through to receive the gift being offered. GOD is continually offering gifts to His children. Our very existence is a gift. The glory of creation that surrounds us is a gift. The people that love us. Gift. Yet it is the miraculous that is so often missed or unseen or passed off as coincidence. This book is a challenge to awareness. To see with spiritual eyes, that which has always been present for you.

I am learning to be HOLY. As I see it, right now, I am just WHOLLY.

Wholly HIS, and I will leave it to him to work out the extra letters on my journey to becoming holy as He is Holy.

THE END? No, THE BEGINNING…

In the kingdom, there are only beginnings.

About the Author

Larissa Kay Ellis is fearless in sharing where she has walked both before and after she met this GOD everyone talks about but so few seem to know intimately. He showed up in her life, miraculously rescuing her, time after time, long before she fell in love with Him. Healed of metastatic cancer in a documented "white light miracle" in 1989, she has written her account of a thirty-three-year mystical journey full of heartbreak, life-threatening "hits," encounters with evil, and divine intervention. Healing, divine appointments, spectacularly answered prayers and miraculous encounters with JESUS himself compelled others to encourage her to write her story.